The Remittance Market in India

The Remittance Market
in India

Opportunities, Challenges, and Policy Options

by

Gabi G. Afram

THE WORLD BANK
Washington, D.C.

© 2012 International Bank for Reconstruction and Development /
International Development Association or The World Bank
1818 H Street NW
Washington DC 20433
Telephone: 202-473-1000
Internet: www.worldbank.org

1 2 3 4 14 13 12 11

ISBN (paper): 978-0-8213-8972-0
ISBN (electronic): 978-0-8213-8934-8
DOI: 10.1596/978-0-8213-8972-0

The Library of Congress Cataloging-in-Publication Data has been applied for.

The painting on the cover, by Elba Gutierrez, is used courtesy of the World Bank's art collection.

Cover design by Debra Naylor of Naylor Design.

Contents

Figures

Tables

Acknowledgments

This report was prepared by a World Bank team led by Gabi Afram under the guidance of Simon Bell, Ivan Rossignol, and Massimo Cirasino. The report team included Harish Natarajan, Luchia Christova, Carlo Corraza, Mukta Joshi, and Dhruba Purkayastha. The team benefited from the advice and comments of Sanket Mohapatra, Samuel Maimbo, and Mario Guadamillas.

The peer reviewers of this book were Deepak Bhattasali and Dilip Ratha, both of the World Bank. The report benefited from extensive discussions and interactions with, and suggestions and insights from, the Department of Financial Services, Ministry of Finance, Reserve Bank of India, and Ministry of Overseas Indian Affairs, as well as various commercial banks, remittance service providers, and other related institutions in India.

The report has been discussed with the government of India, but the government does not necessarily approve of its contents, especially where the authors have stated their judgment and have made policy recommendations.

Executive Summary

Millions of migrants worldwide send billions of dollars in remittances each year to their families or communities of origin. In many developing countries, remittances are an important source of family and national income and also are the largest source of external financing. Remittances are better targeted at the needs of the poor than foreign aid or foreign direct investment (FDI), as recipients often depend on remittances to cover daily living expenses, to provide a cushion against emergencies, or to make small investments in business or education. Therefore, remittance services should be safe, efficient, and reliable. This can be achieved by increasing competition, enhancing access to payment system infrastructure, improving transparency, and ensuring a sound and predictable legal and regulatory framework.

With an estimated US$49 billion in remittance inflows in 2009, India is the world's foremost remittance destination. The size and potential impact of these inflows is large. Despite substantial progress over the past 15 years, the provision of accessible, efficient, safe, and cost-effective remittance services in India could be improved. This report undertakes a broad, detailed diagnostic of the Indian remittance market and analyze its characteristics based on the General Principles for International Remittance Services (GPs). It identifies some of the key actions and public policy measures (especially in the areas of consumer protection, transparency, retail payments, competition, and risk management) for the improvement and future development of this market that would make it more contestable, transparent, accessible, and sound.

Migration from India

Understanding migration patterns and characteristics of migrants is crucial for identifying important remittance channels and designing policy interventions to enhance the remittance market. According to the Ministry of Overseas Indian Affairs (MOIA), India has the second largest Diaspora in the world, with around 25 million people living in some 110 countries. Overseas Indians are divided into Nonresident Indians (NRIs) and People of Indian Origin (PIOs). Migration from India has had three distinct phases: (a) early migration of unskilled labor to work on mines and plantations in British colonies, (b) the late-20th-century migration of unskilled and semiskilled workers to Gulf countries, and (c) the recent migration of high-skilled professional workers to industrial countries.

Although overseas Indians are a socially and economically diverse group of people, some general observations can be made about outward migration from India.

1. The bulk of migration is low skilled in nature. However, more recently, high-skilled migration has picked up and has become increasingly considerable.
2. There are three major destination markets for migrants from India: English-speaking industrial countries, including Australia, Canada, the United Kingdom, and the United States; Gulf countries such as Bahrain, Kuwait, Oman, Qatar, Saudi Arabia, and the United Arab Emirates; and Southeast Asian countries, including Indonesia, Malaysia, Singapore, and Thailand.
3. Migration in the case of the Middle East and Southeast Asia is often temporary, while it tends to be more permanent in the case of the industrial countries.
4. Skill and occupation profile of migrants varies according to the destination. Migration to industrial countries is dominated by high-skilled professional migrants. Migrants to the Middle East and Asia are mainly unskilled and semiskilled workers and some professionals.

India has been one of the few countries in the world to leverage its large Diaspora by successfully issuing Diaspora bonds to tap into the NRIs' assets in 1991, 1998, and 2000. These bonds provided the NRIs with a higher return on their investment compared with similar instruments in their countries of residence. The funds raised from the Diaspora typically are used to face crisis situations as well as to finance long-term investments in infrastructure or projects with high social value.

Remittance Flows to India

The Reserve Bank of India (RBI) reports that workers' remittances to India reached US$46.4 billion for fiscal year (FY) 2008/09 up from US$2.1 billion in FY 1990/91. India, indeed, has overtaken Mexico to become the world's foremost remittance destination. Remittances, which have constituted around 3 to 4 percent of India's gross domestic product (GDP) since 1999–2000, have provided considerable support to India's balance of payments. Remittances also have surpassed both foreign aid flows and FDI flows to India. A large number of Indian households (around 4.5 percent) receive remittances. According to the RBI, more than half of these remittances are utilized for family maintenance (that is, to meet the requirements of migrant's families regarding food, education, health, and other needs) while the rest are either deposited in bank accounts (20 percent) or invested in land, property, and securities (7 percent).

In addition to the improvements in the data collection methods on remittances of recent years, several factors account for this remarkable increase in workers' remittances over the past 15 years. First, in the 1990s, migration of skilled Indian labor to North America increased significantly, particularly among information technology (IT) workers. Second, this increase in immigrant labor coincided with better incentives to send and invest money, relaxed regulations and controls, more flexible exchange rates, and gradual opening of the capital account after 1993. Finally, NRIs have responded well to several attractive deposit schemes in India.

Despite growing by 34 percent in 2008, remittance flows to India started slowing down in the last quarter of 2008 because of the global financial crisis. During the first quarter of 2009, these flows witnessed a sharp decline of 32 percent compared with the same period in 2008. Remittance flows picked up again, however, registering a growth of 5 percent and 4 percent, respectively, in both the second and third quarters of 2009 over the same period in 2008. Indeed, overall remittance flows increased by around 20 percent in FY 2009/10 over the previous fiscal year. This limited effect of the financial crisis on remittance flows to India can be attributed to many reasons. First, India became an attractive investment destination for migrants' savings because of falling asset prices, rising interest rate differentials, and the depreciating rupee. Second, some Indian migrants returned home with their savings or stayed in their destination countries, but sent their families (and savings) home to cope with economic uncertainty. Finally, even though overall employment in high-income countries has declined, the employment prospects of Indian migrants in these countries remained relatively stable during 2008 and 2009. Employment in the sectors in which they are engaged (health care, professional, and technical services) has remained relatively stable compared with the hard-hit construction and real estate sectors.

Remittance transfers often can be costly relative to the low incomes of remitters and the small amounts involved. Various studies over the past eight years have shown that although the costs of sending remittances to India through banks or Money Transfer Operators (MTOs) have been declining over time, it was cheaper to use unofficial methods. The Global Remittance Price database (World Bank 2010b) shows that, for all remittance channels to India, the costs of sending remittances decline with the amount sent. The costs of sending remittances to India are the lowest for Saudi Arabia, Singapore, and the United Arab Emirates, while they are the highest for Canada. Prices of remittance transfers to India differ depending on several factors: sending country, remittance sending scheme, and type of remittance service provider (RSP). Prices were in the range of US$0 to US$5 (plus a foreign exchange [FX] fee) for remittances from Gulf Cooperation Council (GCC) countries using bank-led schemes and US$5 to US$10 (plus the FX fee) for remittances from most countries using MTOs. As for Internet money transfer services for remittances from Canada, Singapore, the United Kingdom, and the United States, the prices ranged from US$0 to US$5 (plus the FX fee). Although the speed of delivering remittances to the recipient depends on the remittance-sending scheme, the location of the recipient, and the type of transfer (cash or account), the delivery times have been shortening and now vary from instant delivery to five days (see table 3.2).

Provision of remittances through banking channels can expand financial inclusion. Remittances can act as a catalyst for individuals to start a relationship and, in turn, build a credit history with a financial institution. With access to savings, insurance, and credit facilities, poor households can better manage their risks. Most remittance-receiving households in India reported receiving these remittances in cash. Financial institutions in India have not yet taken active steps to expand outreach through remittance-linked financial products. Some banks in India are offering special remittance savings accounts; however, none of these banks are providing any special remittance-linked loan products. Remittances can be leveraged to improve financial access by improving migrants' access to bank accounts, designing appropriate remittance-linked products, and using technology to provide remittance and financial services.

The Remittance Market in India

The remittance market in India is serviced by commercial banks, nonbank MTOs, foreign exchange bureaus, cooperative banks, and India Post, as well as a wide variety of commercial entities acting as correspondent agents (subagents). Many of these entities enter into commercial arrangements with exchange houses and other entities in the sending countries to source remittances from the migrants. Banks have the largest share of recorded remittance inflows to India (60 to 80 percent, including Internet-based remittances, which are routed through banks), and MTOs account for the rest. Banks primarily process remittances that are credited to the account of the recipient. The interbank infrastructure used for remittances has played a big role in reducing remittance-processing times and has enabled RSPs to move funds faster to their agents. MTOs such as Western Union (WU), MoneyGram, and others, all operate in India through alliances, partnerships, and subagencies. India Post offers various remittance-related facilities, such as international money transfers, and has partnered with WU to support the transfer of funds using its network. Finally, with the increasing use of technology among financial service providers, Internet-based provision of remittance services is a fast-growing business.

As in other South Asian countries, community-based arrangements for remittance transfers also are used in India. These arrangements include courier transfers, in-kind remittances, and *hawala/hundi*. The characteristics of *hawala* money transfers (predominantly used in the Middle East and South Asia) include ease of operation, lower transaction costs, speed, potential anonymity, and convenience, which explains their usage even today. Although the exact amount of remittances transferred though the *hawala* system is difficult to measure, some studies estimate that the *hawala* market in India could be as large as 30 to 40 percent of the recorded remittance transfers.

All foreign exchange transactions conducted by Indian entities need to conform to the Foreign Exchange Management Act (FEMA) of 1999. FEMA requires business entities wishing to offer foreign currency–related services to obtain a license under any one of four specific categories. These licensing categories are called Authorized Dealers (ADs) I to III and Full-Fledged Money Changers (FFMCs). These four categories cover a variety of institutions, including banks, foreign exchange dealers, MTOs, and specialized financial institutions. Only entities having an AD I or II or FFMC license can offer remittance services directly (see chapter 3 for an explanation of the categories). These entities, however, are required to seek express approval from the Foreign Exchange (FX) Department of RBI to offer remittance services. The FX Department has created two approval regimes for administering the approval process for remittance services: the Rupee Drawing Arrangement (RDA) and the Money Transfer Service Scheme (MTSS).

Remittance services are considered a permitted banking activity; hence, banks have a general permission available to provide remittance services. However, this permission only allows conduct of remittance business in partnership with other domestic banks or with banks in sending countries. Banks in India offering remittance services in partnership with nonbanks in the sending countries need to seek RBI approval under an RDA. In addition, AD I banks and AD IIs, as well as FFMCs, are allowed to offer remittance services directly conforming to the MTSS but also require RBI approval. Under MTSS, all these institutions can offer remittance services in partnership with MTOs, like WU and Money Gram, that provide money transfer services. Indeed, under the same scheme, many commercial banks in India have partnered with MTOs to offer remittance services. Entities licensed under the MTSS can engage other entities as subagents for disbursement of remittances.

Drawing on these two approval regimes, commercial banks and other ADs and FFMCs in India have created five distinct operational schemes for remittance services. These schemes are described in detail in chapter 3 and include bank-operated scheme (RDA), bank-operated scheme (tie-up with foreign bank), Internet-based remittance services, MTO service, and wire transfers.

Diagnostic of the Remittance Market in India

This section summarizes the market for the provision of remittance services in India on the basis of GPs, which is reviewed in chapter 4. It also summarizes the main observations for the future development of this market.

Transparency and Consumer Protection

The market for remittances in India appears to be transparent and the consumers are informed on the different aspects of the transaction. Bank-operated remittance services are subject to the general customer protection and transparency measures specified by the RBI for all banking transactions. The MTSS does not prescribe any specific customer protection and transparency measures. The level of complaints and disputes, however, has been very low and is primarily linked to mistakes in the transcription of recipient's account details and to cash shortage. In the case of unresolved issues, bank customers can approach the banking ombudsman; in addition, the usual legal resolutions schemes are available.

To further enhance transparency and consumer protection in India's market for remittance services, RSPs could be required (as part of the RDA and MTSS approvals) to (a) adopt a consumer protection charter, which is widely publicized; and (b) designate grievance handling officers and publicize their contact details. The authorities could consider extending the ombudsman service to cover MTO-operated schemes to ensure the same level of customer protection for users of MTO services.

Payment System Infrastructure

The existing payment infrastructure offers a range of instruments for cross-border transfers and domestic disbursement of worker remittances. Inward remittances to India largely rely on the banking channels for the disbursement of funds to the recipients. MTOs use an extensive network of bank agents. Banks themselves are active in the remittance market in India. The existence of efficient interbank payment mechanisms has played an enabling role. The bank-operated schemes use the National Electronic Funds Transfer (NEFT) platform to transfer funds to a recipient who does not have a banking relationship with the bank that sourced the remittance. The MTOs use the NEFT platform to move funds to their agents. The MTOs are not participants in the platform. The MTOs operate accounts at commercial banks, and these banks offer fund transfer services to the MTOs. The coverage of electronic retail payment systems is limited in rural and remote areas. Other alternatives are available but not on a large scale.

To increase the proportion of remittance inflows into a bank account, one needs an adequate banking infrastructure (NEFT-enabled or Real-Time Gross Settlement–enabled branches) in areas with a high density of recipients. This infrastructure would enable the local banks to receive and disburse remittances in an efficient way and help reduce the cash payout of remittances, which requires maintaining an agent network. In certain remote areas with underdeveloped telecommunication infrastructure, it is recommended to explore the possibility of allowing business correspondents to disburse remittances. In addition, the authorities should encourage the automation of India Post's branches and encourage them to use the available payment infrastructure to offer remittance payment services in those remote rural areas where banks or nonbank remittance providers are not present.

The RBI could explore with RSPs the feasibility of creating a common infrastructure for the exchange of remittance instructions in the existing payment platforms, for example, NEFT operated by RBI. This infrastructure could be made available to banks and nonbank RSPs. It would increase competition and enable these RSPs to significantly reduce their operational expenses and thus translate into a reduction in the cost of remittances. RBI could evaluate opportunities to connect India's payment infrastructure with those of major remittance-sending countries. These interconnections would make the remittance process extremely efficient and reduce exchange rate conversion costs (as in the case of the interconnection between Mexico's payment infrastructure and the U.S. Automated Clearing House [ACH] system).

Legal and Regulatory Environment

The legislation most relevant to international remittances is FEMA (1999). As of July 2009, 40 banks in collaboration with 70 exchange houses in foreign countries were authorized to operate under the RDA scheme, and 11 overseas principals in collaboration with 26 Indian principal agents were permitted to offer remittance services under the MTSS. The number of subagents exceeds 100,000, including branches of the commercial banks. Inward cash-to-cash or account-to-cash remittances (under the MTSS) that can be received by a single individual are limited to 12 payments a year of amounts not exceeding US$2,500 per payment.

In addition, a ceiling of rupees (Rs) 50,000 is set on the amount that can be paid out in cash. Any amount exceeding this limit has to be paid by check, draft, or payment order, or has to be credited directly to the beneficiary's account. The RBI also prohibits nonbanks from offering domestic remittance services; only banks and post offices are allowed to offer domestic remittance services.

The RBI could review the limits on the frequency of remittance inflows through the MTSS to ensure that they meet the needs of the users. This limit might be prohibitive, for example, in the case when a beneficiary receives remittances from more than one family member working abroad. Given that an industry-wide record of the remittances received does not exist, it is impossible to enforce this requirement, which could force senders to use another MTO even if their preferred MTO offers a better price when one exceeds the limit.

The RBI could evaluate opportunities for leveraging the agent networks of MTOs for domestic remittances. India experiences significant domestic migration, which has created demand for domestic remittance services. The domestic remittance market is serviced only by banks and India Post. The money transfer services of post offices are used quite extensively, but they remain unpopular for time-critical transfers. The unbanked internal migrants rely on community arrangements that often involve the physical transportation of cash.

Market Structure and Competition

The remittance services offered by the banks are geared toward remittances into bank accounts whereas those offered by MTOs are geared toward cash payouts to the recipient. Remittances initiated using bank-operated schemes tend to be larger in size and less frequent than those initiated through the MTOs. The profile of the senders using the bank-operated schemes tends to be skewed toward white-collar workers, whereas the typical sender using an MTO-operated scheme is a blue-collar worker. Given these distinct customer segments and the reluctance of banks to offer cash-to-cash services, the bank-operated and MTO-operated schemes generally are seen as different products, and not as competing products. The authorities could consider creating an enabling framework for banks to offer cash-to-cash services too.

The level of competition is very high in the bank-operated schemes, with many banks active in the market. The level of competition in the MTO segment is very limited, with WU dominating it with close to 80 percent of the market. MoneyGram and the UAE Exchange are also active players in the MTO segment. Some of the international MTOs require their agents to contractually agree on exclusivity, whereby the agent is prohibited from becoming an agent for another MTO. This exclusivity could enable the MTO, which has locked in large agent networks, to charge higher prices for the remittance services and impedes the ability of other MTOs to expand their agent network. The RBI and the Competition Commission of India could study the impact of exclusivity agreements and consider banning these agreements.

Governance and Risk Management

The Foreign Exchange Department of the RBI is responsible for the oversight of the remittances market. Commercial banks, cooperative banks, and nonbanks are supervised by different departments of the RBI. These supervisory departments are tasked with ensuring adherence to the guidelines set by the FX Department for conduct of remittance business under the RDA and MTSSs. The Prevention of Money Laundering Act (PMLA) of 2002 requires all banks to adhere to Combating the Financing of Terrorism and Anti-Money Laundering requirements. PMLA has been amended subsequently, and its present form requires all MTOs to adhere to the same requirements. Proportionally relaxed Know Your Customer requirements are in place for cash-to-cash transactions under Rs 50,000 (approximately US$1,000). Banks are required to submit regular statistical information and to report to the RBI any new subagent agreements.

The RBI currently has detailed guidelines relating to governance and risk management for commercial banks regarding their banking operations, which also covers remittance services. No specific guidelines are issued for the MTSS principal agents, however. The nonbank MTSS principal agents have designed certain in-house mechanisms. To ensure certain minimum standards for governance and risk management, the RBI should consider developing relevant guidelines for the nonbank MTSS principal agents, as well, which would (a) require MTSS principal agents to have a risk management policy for operational, liquidity, and credit risks; (b) require MTSS principal agents to establish policies for enrolling, training, and monitoring their subagents; and (c) require MTSS principal agents to audit their agents and subagents periodically and make them responsible for compliance with all prevalent rules.

The Role of Remittance Service Provider

There is some degree of cooperation among banks in India through the Indian Banks Association (IBA). For the nonbank remittances business, the MTSS principal agents in India do not have any association. Given that all principal agents are also Full-Fledged Money Changers or Banks, the Foreign Exchange Dealers Association of India (FEDAI) and IBA occasionally are consulted to discuss issues relating to money transfer service.

All RSPs should consider developing industry-wide common minimum standards and encourage all agents to have appropriate governance structures in place. Some important aspects that should be covered include (a) transaction timelines; (b) details to be included in receipts; (c) disclosure of exchange rates and fees; (d) complaint procedures and resolution schemes, including the consequences of exceeding transfer times; (e) safety measures, including due provisions to safeguard customer funds that are in the pipeline; and (f) risk management measures. RSPs should undertake efforts to weed out agents perpetrating fraud through a blacklisting mechanism.

The Role of Public Authorities

In India, different aspects of remittance-related activities fall under the jurisdiction of various authorities, such as the RBI, the Ministry of Finance (MoF), and the MOIA. The RBI and MOIA could collaborate in the production and publication of tables with comparative information on costs and other relevant variables relating to remittance services. The RBI could consider evaluating opportunities to increase the scope of data collection related to remittances and to increase the analysis and synthesis of the data collected; the MOIA could consider stepping up its remittance-related data collection from migrants and their families. Finally, to further leverage India's large Diaspora, the Indian authorities can resume their issuance of Diaspora bonds to finance social development and infrastructure projects in India.

The table on the next page summarizes the report's recommendations.

Summary of Recommendations

General principle	Recommendations
Transparency and Consumer Protection	1. RSPs could be required to (a) adopt a consumer protection charter that is widely publicized, (b) designate grievance handling officers, and (c) publicize their contact details.
	2. The authorities could also consider extending the Ombudsman service to cover MTO-operated scheme.
Payment Systems Infrastructure	3. There should be adequate banking infrastructure (NEFT/RTGS enabled branches) in the areas with high density of recipients.
	4. In certain remote areas with underdeveloped telecommunication infrastructure, banks should actively explore the possibility of using business correspondents to disburse remittances.
	5. The authorities should encourage the automation of India Post's branches.
	6. RBI could explore with RSPs the feasibility of creating a common infrastructure for exchange of remittance instructions in the existing payment platforms like NEFT operated by RBI.
	7. RBI could evaluate opportunities to connect India's payment infrastructure with those of major remittance sending countries.
Legal and Regulatory Framework	8. RBI could consider reviewing the limits on the frequency of remittance inflows through the MTSS to ensure that they meet the needs of the users.
	9. RBI could evaluate opportunities for leveraging the agent networks of MTOs for domestic remittances.
Market Structure and Competition	10. RBI and the Competition Commission of India could study the impact of exclusivity agreements and consider banning them.
Governance and Risk Management	11. RBI could consider developing a guideline on the governance and risk management requirements to be followed by nonbank MTOs.
Role of RSPs	12. RSPs should consider developing industry-wide common minimum standards and encourage all agents to have appropriate governance structures in place.
Role of Public Authorities	13. RBI and MOIA could collaborate in the production and publication of tables with comparative information on costs and other relevant variables relating to remittance services.
	14. RBI could consider evaluating opportunities to increase the scope of data collection related to remittances.
	15. MOIA could consider stepping up its remittance-related data collection from migrants and their families.
	16. Indian authorities can resume their issuance of Diaspora bonds to finance social development and infrastructure projects in India.

(continued next page)

Summary of Recommendations *(continued)*

General principle	Recommendations
Increasing Financial Access through Remittances	17. Migrants' access to bank accounts can be improved by issuing identification cards and by encouraging source country banks to open branches in destination countries.
	18. Development of appropriate financial products can bring low-income recipients, especially unbanked ones, into the financial system. The authorities can offer incentives to financial institutions by considering remittance-linked loan products for unbanked customers as priority sector lending or subject to lower provisioning requirements.
	19. Indian policy makers can exploit the wide usage of mobile phones by promoting new partnerships and linkages between financial institutions and mobile phone operators.

Note: RBI = Reserve Bank of India; RSP = Remittance Service Provider; RTGS = Real-Time Gross Settlement; MOIA = Ministry of Overseas Indian Affairs; MTO = Money Transfer Operator; NEFT = National Electronic Funds Transfer.

List of Abbreviations

ACH	Automated Clearing House
AD	Authorized Dealer
ADB	Asian Development Bank
AML	Anti-Money Laundering
ATM	automated teller machine
BCs	business correspondents
CCI	Competition Commission of India
CFT	Combating the Financing of Terrorism
CPSS	Committee for Payment and Settlement Systems
DFS	Department of Financial Services
ECS	Electronic Clearing Service
FATF	Financial Action Task Force
FCNR(A)	Foreign Currency Nonresident (Accounts)
FCNR(B)	Foreign Currency Nonresident–Bank
FDI	foreign direct investment
FEDAI	Foreign Exchange Dealers Association of India
FEMA	Foreign Exchange Management Act
FIU	Financial Intelligence Unit
FFMC	Full-Fledged Money Changer
FY	fiscal year

FX	foreign exchange
GCC	Gulf Cooperation Council
GDP	gross domestic product
GNI	gross national income
GoI	Government of India
GPs	General Principles for International Remittance Services
IADB	Inter-American Development Bank
IBA	Indian Banks Association
ICT	information communications technology
IDRBT	Institute for Development and Research in Banking Technology
IHDS	India Human Development Survey
ILO	International Labour Organization
KYC	Know Your Customer
MFI	microfinance institution
MO	Money Order
MoF	Ministry of Finance
MOIA	Ministry of Overseas Indian Affairs
MTOs	Money Transfer Operators
MTSS	Money Transfer Service Scheme
NABARD	National Bank for Agriculture and Rural Development
NEFT	National Electronic Funds Transfer
NFS	National Financial Switch
NGO	nongovernmental organization
NPCIL	National Payment Corporation of India Limited
NR(E)RA	Nonresident (External) Rupee Account
NRIs	Nonresident Indians
NR (NR) RD	Nonresident (Nonrepatriable) Rupee Deposits
NRO	Nonresident Ordinary
OECD	Organisation for Economic Co-operation and Development
PAN	Permanent Account Number
PIO	People of Indian Origin
PMEAC	Economic Advisory Council to the Prime Minister
PMLA	Prevention of Money Laundering Act
PO	postal order
POS	point of sale
P&SSA	Payments and Settlement Systems Act of 2007
RBI	Reserve Bank of India

RDA	Rupee Drawing Arrangement
Rs	Indian rupees
RSPs	remittance service providers
RTGS	Real-Time Gross Settlement
SBI	State Bank of India
SWIFT	Society for Worldwide Interbank Financial Telecommunications
US$	U.S. dollars
UTN	unique transaction number
WU	Western Union

Introduction

Importance of Remittances

Millions of migrants send remittances to their families and communities of origin. Worldwide, remittances are estimated to have totaled US$414 billion in 2009, of which US$316 billion went to developing countries, and involved about 192 million migrants or approximately 3 percent of the world population.[1] In many developing countries, remittances are an important source of family (and national) income and are the largest source of external financing. Indeed, in certain developing countries, remittances can account for more than 20 percent of GDP (see figure 1).

The size and potential impact of the remittance inflows is large. Remittances increase the recipient country's foreign exchange reserves. Although capital flows tend to increase during favorable economic cycles and decline in bad times, remittances tend to be countercyclical relative to recipient countries' economic cycles. Remittances also tend to be less volatile than other sources of foreign exchange earnings. Remittances support financial sector development through a strong and positive impact on bank deposits and credit to the private sector.

At the household level, the recipients often depend on remittances to cover daily living expenses, to provide a cushion against emergencies,

Figure 1   Countries with Highest Remittances as a Share of GDP in 2008

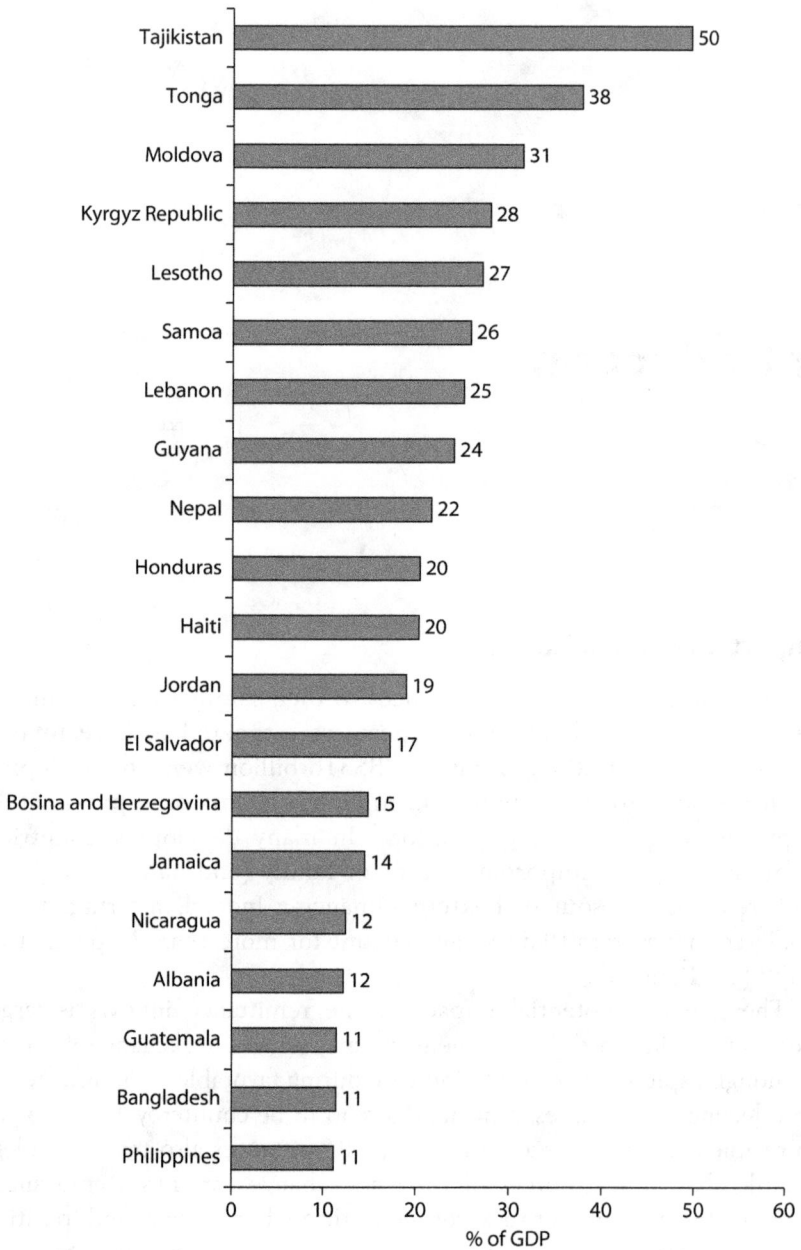

Source: World Bank 2010.

or to make small investments in business or education. Remittances are better targeted to the needs of the poor than are foreign aid or foreign direct investment. In addition, because most remittances tend to be used for consumption rather than investment, they do not respond much to the change in relative rates of return on investments in remittance-receiving countries (although the second round effect on investment is positive, as the rising consumption demand gives a boost to production) (Gupta 2006).

Despite a slowdown in overall remittance flows to developing countries because of the global financial crisis, remittance flows to South Asia have been resilient. In fact, remittance flows to India remained stable in 2009 (notwithstanding a decline in the first quarter).

Purpose of the Study

International remittance services should be safe, efficient, and reliable. This can be achieved by (a) increasing competition in the remittance industry, (b) providing broader access to payment system infrastructure, (c) enhancing transparency, and (d) ensuring a sound and predictable legal and regulatory framework. Historically, one important obstacle to the improvement of remittance services has been the lack of proper policy guidance on such key areas of the remittance market until the World Bank and the Committee for Payment and Settlement Systems (CPSS) of the Bank for International Settlements (BIS) developed the General Principles for International Remittance Services (GPs) in 2007 (BIS 2007). The GPs share the four aims for improving remittance services.

With an estimated US$49 billion in remittance inflows in 2009, India is the world's foremost remittance destination. The size and potential impact of these inflows is large. Despite substantial progress over the past 15 years, the provision of accessible, efficient, and cost-effective remittance services in India could be improved. Remittance transfers often can be costly relative to the low incomes of remitters and the small amounts involved, especially in rural India, and may not be accessible. Attempts to examine the remittance market in India have been limited, however, and mostly have focused on specific issues.

This report attempts to fill the gap by undertaking a broad, detailed investigation of the Indian remittance market and by analyzing its characteristics based on the GPs. It identifies some of the key actions and public policy measures for the improvement and future development of this market, which would make it more contestable, transparent, accessible, and sound. Such actions and policy measures could assist financial institutions and policy makers in enhancing the safety and efficiency of, as well as lowering the costs of, remittance services in India. The World Bank, together with other development organizations, has been involved in promoting and supporting similar studies in other parts of the world.

In chapter 1, this report maps the patterns and characteristics of migration flows from India; in chapter 2, it provides a detailed discussion of remittance flows to India in terms of their importance, sources, uses, trends, costs, and links to financial access. In chapter 3, the report describes the remittance market (the players, the regulatory framework, as well as the existing operational schemes), setting the stage for chapter 4, which presents a diagnostic of the remittance market based on the GPs. The diagnostic covers the legal and regulatory framework, payment system infrastructure, market transparency and level of consumer protection, market structure, level of competition among remittance service providers, as well as market governance. It analyzes the existing situation in India and provides detailed recommendations (including lessons learned from international best practices) that are aimed at increasing competition in the remittance industry, providing broader access to payment system infrastructure, enhancing transparency, and ensuring a sound and predictable legal and regulatory framework. Several of the proposed actions could set a basis for leveraging remittances to achieve other important public policy goals such as broadening financial access, expanding financial inclusion, and both strengthening and deepening the financial sector.

The report was prepared through (a) background research (data research and mining, literature review, collection of relevant material and information, and background research), (b) a field visit in 2009 (a team of experts visited India and conducted interviews and focus groups with all relevant stakeholders and major institutions active in the remittance market), and (c) surveys of both the authorities and the market players.

Note

1. Down from US$338 billion in 2008 (World Bank 2009, 2010).

References

BIS (Bank for International Settlements). 2007. "General Principles for International Remittance Services." Committee on Payment and Settlement Systems Publication 76, BIS Basel, Switzerland.

Gupta, P. 2006. "Macroeconomic Determinants of Remittances: Evidence from India." Working Paper 05/224, International Monetary Fund, Washington, DC.

World Bank. 2009. "Migration and Development Brief 11." World Bank, Washington, DC.

———. 2010. "Migration and Development Brief 12." World Bank, Washington, DC.

CHAPTER 1

Migration from India: Patterns and Characteristics

Understanding migration patterns and the characteristics of migrants is crucial for identifying important remittance channels and designing policy interventions to enhance the remittance market. This chapter analyzes the migration patterns from India over time and also identifies characteristics and profiles of migrants from India to important destination countries. This chapter sets the stage for the discussion on the remittance market in India, as the profile of migrants and their migration destinations have a lot of bearing on the types of remittance instruments they use and the amounts of remittances they send to India, which consequently affect the sort of interventions designed to enhance the remittance market.

Migration from India

Accurate data on migration are not readily available for the majority of the countries in the world, and India is no exception. Data on migration involve two elements: migration stock abroad (the overall size of the Diaspora at a certain point in time) and migration flows from India. The stock of migrants abroad changes not only with new migration flows, but also with returning migration. Migrant population estimates for India differ from one source to the other. Available data show that the Canada,

Malaysia, Saudi Arabia, the United Arab Emirates, the United Kingdom, and the United States are the most important countries for outward migration from India, while the neighboring South Asian countries of Bangladesh, Nepal, Pakistan, and Sri Lanka are the most prominent sources of inward migration to India (see appendix A for a discussion of migration to India).

According to the Ministry of Overseas Indian Affairs (MOIA), India has the second-largest Diaspora in the world, with around 25 million people living in some 110 countries (MOIA 2009).[1] The Overseas Indians are divided into Nonresident Indians (NRIs), whose main destination countries are Bangladesh, Canada, Kuwait, Nepal, Oman, Qatar, Saudi Arabia, Sri Lanka, the United Arab Emirates, the United Kingdom, and the United States, and People of Indian Origin (PIOs),[2] who live permanently in countries like Malaysia, Mauritius, and Myanmar[3] and have constituted established communities in those countries for a long time. MOIA estimates that 5 million people out of the total Diaspora live in the Gulf countries. The World Bank estimates the stock of migrants from India amounted to around 10 million people in 2005, making India the third most important source country for labor migration in the world (see figure 1.1). It is not easy to quantify the number of illegal Indian migrants abroad. Unlike other big migration-source countries, however, the numbers of illegal Indian migrants are not high given the size of the Diaspora. Industry sources estimate that number at around 250,000 to 300,000 people.

After independence, migration from India has been dominated by the flow of migrant workers going to the Gulf countries (mainly to Saudi Arabia and the United Arab Emirates) in the 1970s and 1980s. However, the migration of skilled professionals, especially information technology (IT) workers, to the United States has been the trend since the 1990s. Canada is another important member country of the Organisation of Economic Co-operation and Development (OECD) with a large Indian migrant population. In addition, Indian workers also have migrated to Europe in search of better opportunities. Given its colonial ties with the United Kingdom, most Indian migration to Europe is concentrated in the United Kingdom. Indian migration to Australia, Canada, Europe, and the United States has doubled between 1996 and 2006. In the East Asia region, most migration from India is to Malaysia. Figure 1.2 plots the major regional destinations for Indian migrants abroad. Gulf Cooperation Council (GCC) countries[4] account for 42 percent of the total, and around one-fifth of Indian migrants live in other South Asian countries. About 12 percent reside in the United States (Mohapatra and Ratha 2009).

Figure 1.1   Top 10 Emigration Countries

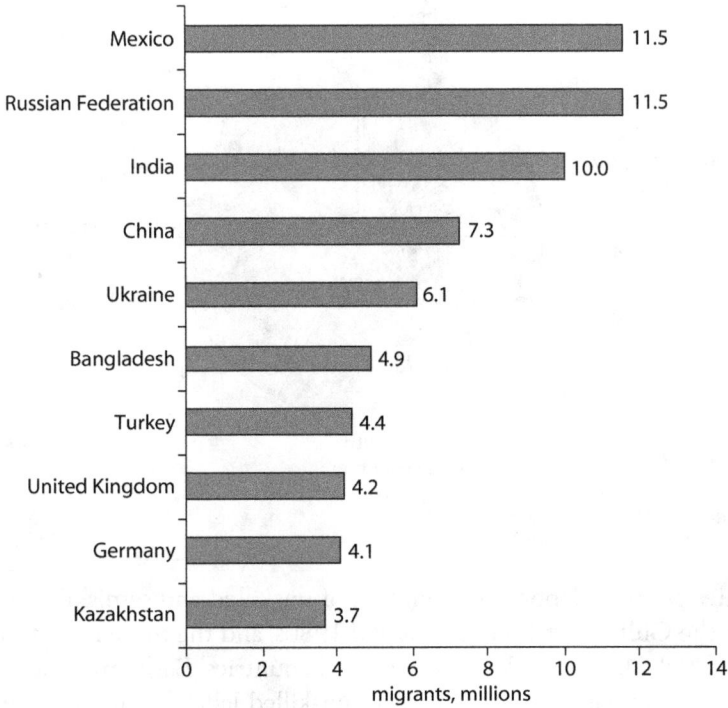

Source: World Bank 2008.
Note: Data are for 2005.

MOIA publishes data for annual labor outflows to those destination countries that require an emigration check.[5] As figure 1.3 shows, the number of such migrants from India increased by around 80 percent over a five-year period to reach around 850,000 workers in 2008. Around 70 percent of these workers migrated to only two countries, namely, Saudi Arabia and the United Arab Emirates.

The Indian states with the highest rate of migrants are Kerala, Tamil Nadu, and Uttar Pradesh, accounting for 53 percent of the total 850,000 workers who received an official clearance to work overseas in 2008.

Profile of Migrants from India

Migration from India has had three distinct phases (which affected the profile of the migrants in each phase): the early migration to British

Figure 1.2   India Migration: Breakdown by Major Region

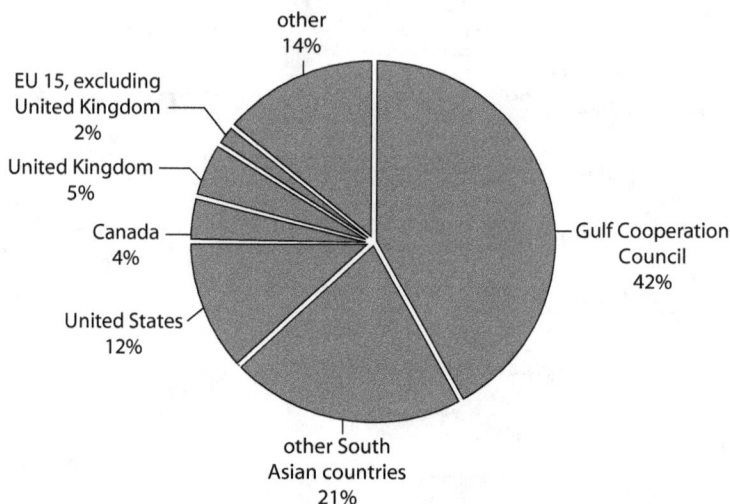

other
14%

EU 15, excluding
United Kingdom
2%

United Kingdom
5%

Canada
4%

United States
12%

Gulf Cooperation
Council
42%

other South
Asian countries
21%

Source: Mohapatra and Ratha 2009.

colonies as cheap labor, the migration of unskilled and semiskilled workers to the Gulf countries in 1970s and 1980s, and the more recent migration of high-skilled workers to industrial countries. Early migration from
India involved large exodus of cheap unskilled labor leaving India in the
19th century to meet the enormous demand for indentured labor in the
British colonies (primarily in the Caribbean, South and East Africa, and
Southeast Asia) for plantation and mining work soon after the British
abolished slavery. The exodus of high-skilled professional workers to the
industrial countries is a post-independence phenomenon, which became
more prominent with the more recent migration of IT workers. In paral-
lel to the migration of high-skilled workers, the 20th century also witnessed the migration of unskilled and semiskilled workers from India to
the Gulf countries.

Overseas Indians are a socially and economically diverse group of
people. Indian migrants' profile cannot be drawn easily, as the range of
income levels and social statuses in the destination countries varies enor-
mously. Professionals, skilled workers, and blue-collar workers are present
in variable percentages in many destination countries. According to
MOIA, Overseas Indians worldwide are estimated to produce an annual
income of about US$400 billion, equivalent to 30 percent of India's GDP.
Still, some general observations can be made about outward migration
from India (Chanda and Sreenivasan 2006):

Figure 1.3   Annual Labor Outflows from India, 2004–08

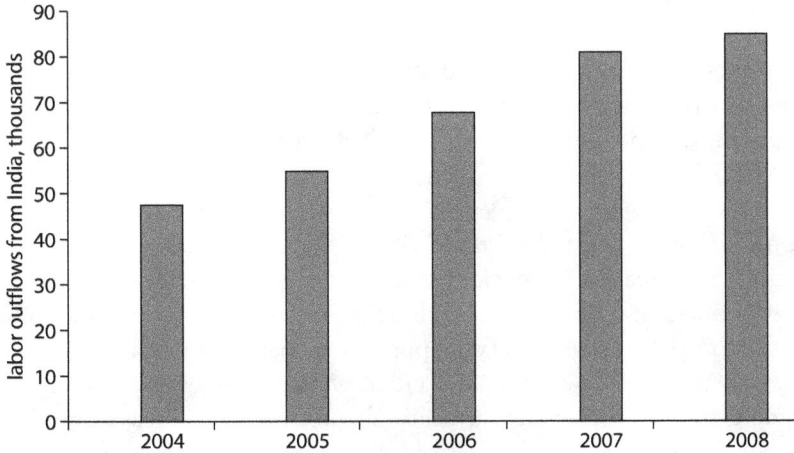

Source: MOIA 2009.

1. The bulk of migration from India is low skilled in nature, in occupations such as transport operations, repair and maintenance, construction, and domestic help. More recently, however, high-skilled migration has picked up.
2. Migrants from India have three major destination markets: English-speaking industrial countries, including Australia, Canada, the United Kingdom, and the United States; Gulf countries, such as Bahrain, Kuwait, Oman, Qatar, Saudi Arabia, and the United Arab Emirates; and Southeast Asian countries, including Indonesia, Malaysia, Singapore, and Thailand.
3. In the case of Middle Eastern and Southeast Asian countries, migration often is temporary, while it tends to be more permanent in the case of the industrial countries.
4. Skill and occupation profiles of the Indian migrants vary according to the destination markets. Migration to the industrial countries is domi-nated by high-skilled professional migrants in the fields of medicine, IT, teaching, and engineering. OECD data for 2000 show that of the Indian migrants to the OECD countries, 22 percent are low skilled, 18 percent are medium skilled, and 60 percent are high skilled.[6] Mi-grants to the Middle East are mainly unskilled or semiskilled workers in construction work, transport operations, and domestic services. Some professionals in health care and accounting are migrating to the Middle

East. Migrants to Southeast Asia are a mix of unskilled and semiskilled workers in plantation and domestic services as well as professionals in health care and IT.

Profiles of Indian migrants to the six major destination countries of Canada, Malaysia, Saudi Arabia, the United Arab Emirates, the United Kingdom, and the United States, as well as the GCC are described below (GoI 2001).

Profile of migrants to the United States. In the United States, the foreign-born population is considered as immigrant population. The immigrant population numbers thus include mainly those who migrated to the United States on a temporary or permanent basis for employment purposes as well as the naturalized citizens. About 44 percent of Indian migrants to the Unites States are naturalized citizens, whereas others hold temporary visas or permanent residency. According to the U.S. Census Bureau, close to 1.1 million Indians were employed in the United States in 2009. Indian migrants are better educated than the native population or other migrants. Only 3.6 percent of Indian migrants had less than a high school education (Mohapatra and Ratha 2009).

Therefore, Indian migrants earn higher incomes than the median salaries of the average American. The per capita income of Indian migrants in 2007 was US$50,000 in inflation-adjusted dollars, whereas the average income of all migrants was US$28,000 and that of natives was US$27,000. The poverty rate for Indian migrants in the United States was 7.2 percent (Camarota 2007). Indeed, according to MOIA, every 10th Indian American is a millionaire and every fifth start-up company in the Silicon Valley is owned by an Indian.

Profile of migrants to Canada. With the foreign-born population considered as an immigrant population, the majority of the immigrant population in Canada constitutes those who migrated to Canada on a temporary or permanent basis for employment purposes. In 2001, 26 percent Indian immigrants in Canada had a university degree, and the average income of Indian migrant in Canada was about 20 percent higher than the national average (Canada Immigrant Job Issues 2006). About 30 percent of migrants had jobs in the professional and management positions, and 23 percent worked in the manufacturing sector. The bulk of the migrants from India to Canada had a mathematics, engineering, or applied sciences background.

Profile of migrants to the United Kingdom. In the United Kingdom, the immigrant population is considered as the foreign resident population and includes those residing in the United Kingdom for permanent or employment purposes. With per capita income higher than the national average, the Indian migrants are among the highest earning groups in the United Kingdom. The Indian community in the United Kingdom accounted for about 40 percent of the retail sector employment, and significant numbers were employed as doctors, general practitioners, and consultants in 2001. With their higher level of education and professional skills, the unemployment rate among the Indian community is much lower than that in other migrant populations.

Profile of migrants to Malaysia. Being engaged mainly in rubber and palm plantation labor, many first-generation Indian migrants to Malaysia were illiterate or had little education. By 2000, however, only about 15 percent of the Indian migrants remained in the agriculture sector, and 62 percent had moved to the manufacturing and services sectors. Indians constitute about 15 percent of the skilled professionals in Malaysia. The average income of an Indian migrant in Malaysia is below that of an average Malaysian.

Profile of migrants to Saudi Arabia. In the wake of oil boom, there has been a steady increase in the employment of Indian nationals in Saudi Arabia. According to the government of India (GoI), about 85 percent of Indian migrants to Saudi Arabia work as organized labor and technicians on project sites and industrial establishments. Close to 10 percent of migrants are employed in white-collar jobs, such as clerks, secretaries, and accountants. Highly qualified professionals such as doctors, engineers, and chartered accountants constitute only 5 percent of the migrant population.

Profile of migrants to the United Arab Emirates. As infrastructure and other developmental projects sprouted in the United Arab Emirates, the introduction of skilled and unskilled labor became a necessity, and India was an obvious choice to supply such labor. In 2001, about 75 percent of migrant Indian workers in the United Arab Emirates were laborers (half of whom were unskilled) and the remaining 25 percent were professionals.

Profile of migrants to the GCC. In the GCC as a whole, most Indian migrants are temporarily employed on a contractual basis, and a large majority (70 percent) of Indian migrants to these countries are unskilled or semiskilled workers. Of the remaining migrants, 20 percent have white-collar jobs and only 10 percent are estimated to be professionals (Bhandari and Malik 2008).

Diaspora Bonds

India has been one of the few countries in the world to leverage its large Diaspora by successfully issuing Diaspora bonds (with the State Bank of India [SBI] as a medium for transactions). It has tapped into the NRIs' assets on three occasions:

1. 1991—India Development Bonds (US$1.6 billion, at 9.5 percent in U.S. dollar terms): following the balance of payment crisis in 1991
2. 1998—Resurgent India Bonds (US$4.2 billion, at 7.75 percent in U.S. dollar terms): following the sanctions imposed after the nuclear explosions in 1998
3. 2000—India Millennium Deposits (US$5.5 billion, at 8.5 percent in U.S. dollar terms)

These bonds provided the NRIs with a higher return on their investment compared with similar instruments in their countries of residence. The bonds (issued in U.S. dollars, British pounds, and deutsche marks/euros) were offered exclusively to NRIs with a five-year bullet maturity. The funds raised from the Diaspora typically are used to face crisis situations, as well as to finance long-term investments in infrastructure or projects with high social value (Ketkar and Ratha 2010).

Notes

1. An International Labour Organization (ILO) study puts the number of Indians living abroad at 20 million (Chanda and Sreenivasan 2006).
2. PIOs include Indian citizens who have migrated to another country, people of Indian origin who were born outside India, or people of Indian origin who reside outside India.
3. An estimated 1.6 million and 2.5 million PIOs live in Malaysia and Myanmar, respectively.
4. The GCC is composed of six countries: Bahrain, Kuwait, Oman, Qatar, Saudi Arabia, and the United Arab Emirates.
5. These data *do not* include migrants to the Australia, Canada, the European Union, the United Kingdom, and the United States, because these destination countries do not require an official clearance.

6. The definitions of low (primary education, 0–8 years of schooling), medium (secondary education, 9–12 years of schooling), and high skilled (tertiary education, 13 or more years of schooling) are as defined by Docquier and Marfouk (2004).

References

Bhandari, L., and P. Malik. 2008. "India's Talent Migration." Prepared for Manpower, Inc., New Delhi, November 8.

Camarota, S. 2007. "Immigrants in the United States 2007: A Profile of America's Foreign Born Population." *Center for Immigration Studies Backgrounder* (November). Background Paper.

Canada Immigrant Job Issues. 2006. "East Indian Immigrants in Canada." Available at http://www.canadaimmigrants.com/qualityoflife/communities/indian.asp (accessed on October 1, 2009).

Chanda, R. and N. Sreenivasan. 2006. "India's Experience with Skilled Migration." In *Competing for Global Talent*, ed. C. Kuptsch and E. F. Pang, 215–56. Geneva: International Institute for Labor Studies.

Docquier, F., and A. Marfouk. 2004. "Measuring the International Mobility of Skilled Workers (1990–2000)." Policy Research Working Paper No. 3381, World Bank, Washington, DC.

GoI (Government of India). 2001. "Report on the Indian Diaspora" High Level Committee on the Indian Diaspora. Available at http://www.indiandiaspora .nic.in/contents.htm (accessed on October 1, 2009).

Ketkar, S., and D. Ratha. 2010. "Diaspora Bonds as a New Funding Vehicle from Developing Countries." Research paper prepared for the Institute for International Law and Justice, New York.

Mohapatra, S., and D. Ratha. 2009. "Impact of Global Financial Crisis on Remittances and Migration in India." World Bank, Washington, DC.

MOIA (Ministry of Overseas Indian Affairs). 2009. *Annual Report 2008–2009*. Available at http://moia.gov.in (accessed October 1, 2009).

World Bank. 2008. *Migration and Remittance Factbook*. Washington, DC: World Bank.

CHAPTER 2

International Remittance Flows to India: Importance, Trends, Costs, and Link to Financial Access

This chapter analyzes the characteristics and importance of international migrant remittance flows to India. The chapter begins by defining and measuring these flows and analyzing their sources and importance to India's economy, as well as their uses at the household level. It then describes the impact of the global financial crisis on these flows and attempts to estimate the overall financial costs involved in the remittance process. Finally, the chapter discusses how these remittances are being leveraged for enhancing financial access in India.

Importance of Remittance Flows to India

The Reserve Bank of India (RBI) reports that workers' remittances to India reached US$46.4 billion for fiscal year (FY) 2008/09 up from US$2.1 billion in FY 1990/91 (see table 2.1)[1]. With a population of more than 1 billion, an active labor force of more than 467 million and a low (although steadily increasing) gross national income (GNI) per capita at US$1,070, emigration to more developed countries constitutes an important and attractive source of income for many Indian workers (World Bank 2008).

Table 2.1   Workers' Remittances to India

Fiscal year	Amount (US$, billions)	% of GDP
1990/91	2.1	0.7
1995/96	8.5	2.4
1999/2000	12.3	2.7
2000/01	13.1	2.8
2001/02	15.8	3.3
2002/03	17.2	3.4
2003/04	22.2	3.7
2004/05	21.1	3.0
2005/06	25.0	3.1
2006/07	30.8	3.4
2007/08	43.5	3.7
2008/09	46.4	4

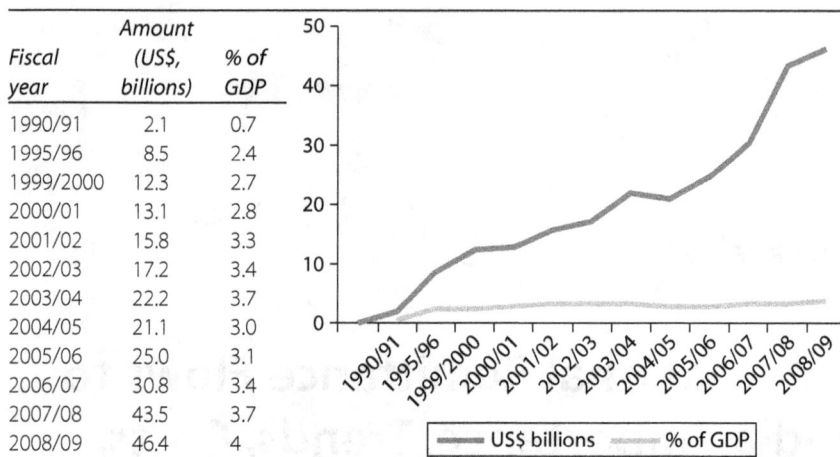

Source: RBI 2010b.

India has overtaken Mexico to become the world's foremost remittance destination. With remittance receipts of 45 billion or more each, India and China are the leading recipients of remittances worldwide. Figure 2.1 presents the top 20 remittance-receiving countries in calendar year 2009, showing India leading the pack.

Workers' remittances, which have constituted around 3 to 4 percent of India's GDP since FY 1999/2000, have provided considerable support to India's balance of payments. Remittances financed about 45 percent of the merchandise trade deficit between FY 2005/06 and FY 2008/09.

Remittances have surpassed both foreign aid flows and foreign direct investment (FDI) flows. Figure 2.2 presents remittance inflows as a share of selected financial flows and GDP to demonstrate the extent to which remittances contribute to a country's foreign exchange reserves. Remittances have been a stable source of funds in India's balance of payments and are not affected by risk-return considerations to the same extent that flows on capital account have been. Moreover, remittances to India tend to be higher when economic conditions in the host countries are favorable and are somewhat countercyclical (Gupta 2006).

A large number of Indian households receive remittances. According to the India Human Development Survey (IHDS) (a nationally representative survey of 215,754 households), around 4.5 percent of Indian households sent or received remittances in 2004–05.[2] The average

Figure 2.1   Top 20 Remittance-Receiving Countries, 2009

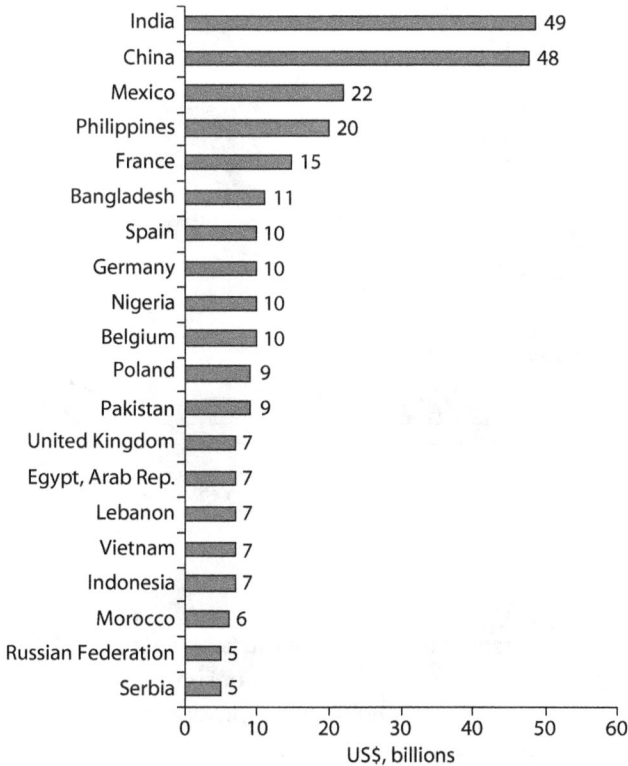

Source: World Bank 2010a.

remittance size was Rs 951.64 (around US$22.5). The proportion of households sending and receiving remittances was relatively higher in rural areas. About 5.2 percent of rural households claimed to send or receive remittances with an average value of Rs 1,025.93, and 3.1 percent urban households sent or received an average value of Rs 804.49 in remittances. The survey did not distinguish between domestic or international remittance receipts.

More than half of the remittances received by Indian households are used for family maintenance, that is, to meet the requirements of migrants' families regarding food, education, health, and so on (61 percent), according to an RBI survey (RBI 2010a). On average, about 20 percent of the funds received are deposited in bank accounts, and about 7 percent of the funds received are invested in land, property, or securities. Although a

Figure 2.2   Remittance Inflows as a Share of Selected Financial Flows and GDP, FY 2008/09

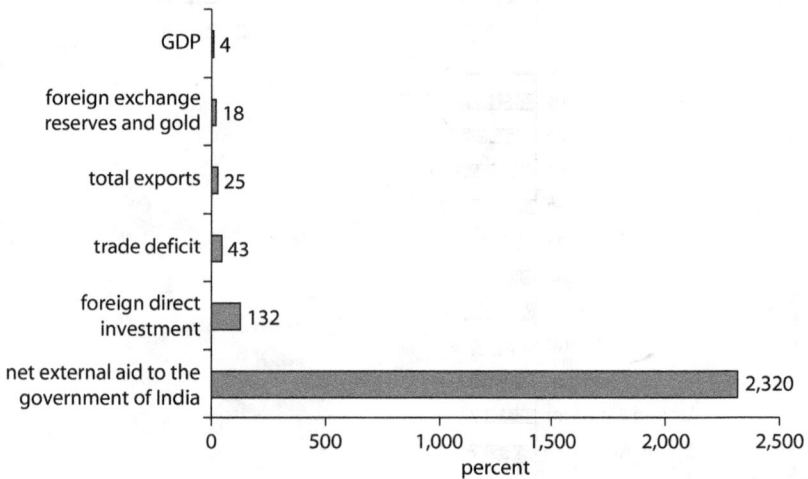

Source: RBI 2010b.

small share of remittances is used for investment, there is a definite second round effect on investment as the rising consumption of remittance-receiving households is likely to boost other productive sectors.

In addition to the improvements in the data collection methods on remittances of recent years, several factors account for this remarkable increase in workers' remittances over the past 15 years. First, in the 1990s, migration of skilled Indian labor to North America increased significantly, particularly among information technology (IT) workers. Second, this increase in migrant labor coincided with better incentives to send and invest money, relaxed regulations and controls, more flexible exchange rates, and the gradual opening of the capital account after 1993. This drastically reduced the use of systems such as *hundi/hawala* to send remittances. Finally, Nonresident Indians (NRIs) have responded well to several attractive deposit schemes.

Sources of Remittance Flows to India

The origin countries for remittance flows to India correspond to the destination countries for Indian migrants. However, estimates of the breakdown of these flows by country or region vary (sometimes substantially)

Figure 2.3   Source Regions of Remittance Flows to India, 2009

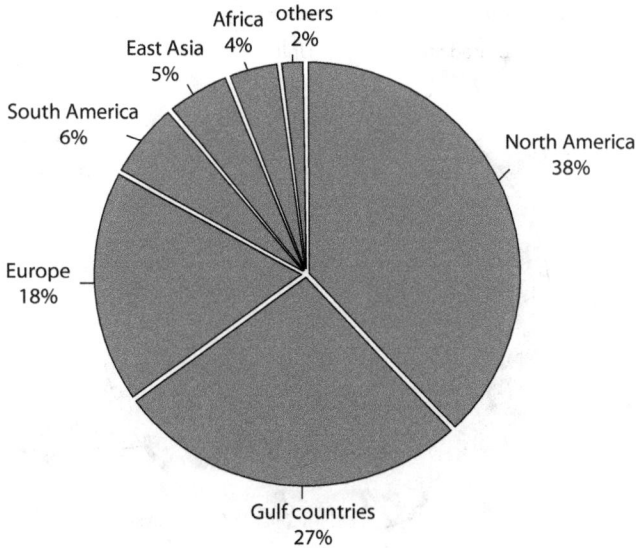

Source: RBI 2010a.

from one source to the other. As can be seen in figure 2.3, the RBI estimates that around 38 percent of total remittances to India in 2009
originated from North America while 27 percent originated from the
Gulf countries, despite the fact that the latter have a much larger Indian
migrant population (RBI 2010a). This could be due to the fact that
Indian migrants to North American tend to be more skilled and higher
paid. It could reflect data recording issues.[3]

World Bank estimates, on the other hand, identify six major country
corridors for Indian migration and remittances (see figure 2.4), which
account for more than 55 percent of migration from India, and 73 percent of remittance flows to India.[4] Gulf countries remain the top destinations for Indian migrants followed by the United States. The
remittances received from Saudi Arabia and the United Arab Emirates
are relatively higher because of the larger migrant populations in these
countries, and the fact that most of the migration to these countries is
temporary and migrants tend to send most of their savings back home
(whereas migrants to the United States are permanently settled and
come from families that need less support; hence they tend to send
relatively lower remittances).[5]

Figure 2.4   Estimates of Migrant Destinations and Remittance Flows

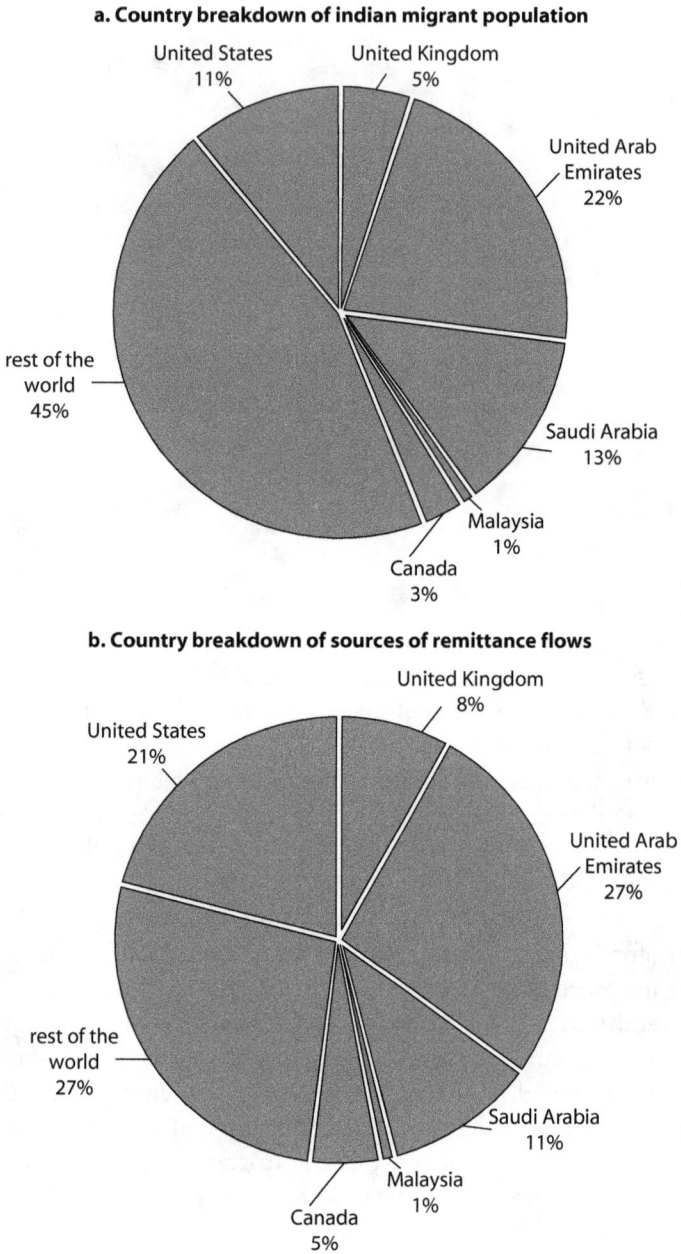

a. Country breakdown of indian migrant population

b. Country breakdown of sources of remittance flows

Source: Ratha and Shaw (2007).

More recently, an unrepresentative survey of leading Indian remittance service providers (RSPs) undertaken for this study showed that North America accounted for 57.5 percent of the volume of incoming remittance flows, followed by the Gulf region with 15.5 percent, East Asia with 11.5 percent, Europe with 8.0 percent, and Australia with 6.5 percent. Finally, the Ministry of Overseas Indian Affairs (MOIA) estimated that around 40 percent of the remittances received in 2008 were from the 5 million overseas Indian workers in the Gulf countries and Malaysia (MOIA 2009). India is also home to a large immigrant population and therefore is a source of remittance outflows (see appendix A for a discussion of outward remittances).

Inward Remittances and NRI Deposit Schemes

According to the RBI, private transfers (or recorded remittances) include inward remittances from Indian workers abroad for family maintenance purposes, local withdrawal from NRI rupee deposits, gold and silver brought through passenger baggage, and personal gifts and donations to charitable and religious institutions. A major part of the outflows from NRI deposits is in the form of local withdrawals that are utilized within India and cease to exist as an external liability in the capital account. Private transfers have been growing over the past years (see table 2.2).

Table 2.2   Composition of Private Transfers to India

US$ billion

Year	Total private transfers	Inward remittances for family maintenance	Local withdrawals/ redemptions from NRI deposits	Local withdrawals/ redemptions from NRI deposits as a percentage of total private transfers	Local withdrawals/ redemptions from NRI deposits as % of total NRI deposit redemptions
			Of which		
2005–06	25.0	10.5	12.5	49.9	82.8
2006–07	30.8	14.7	13.2	42.8	84.7
2007–08 PR	43.5	21.9	18.9	43.5	64.7
2008-09 P	46.4	23.1	20.6	44.5	62.9

Source: RBI 2010b.
Note: PR = Partially Revised; P = Preliminary.

Since 2003–04, the share of local withdrawals in the total private transfers has remained above 40 percent.

Since the 1970s, the government of India (GoI) has introduced special deposit schemes for NRIs to attract foreign capital. NRI deposits can be held in foreign currency denominations or in Indian rupees. Deposits held in foreign denominations are treated like debt because depositors using such accounts can repatriate their principal and interest in foreign currency whenever they choose to do so. Conversely, funds locally withdrawn from rupee-denominated deposit accounts are treated as remittances by the RBI.

The following are the NRI deposit schemes that presently are operational (RBI 2008):

Foreign Currency Nonresident–Bank (FCNR(B)) Account. The deposits under FCNR(B) accounts and the interest earned thereon are maintained in a foreign currency. Deposits under this scheme are repatriable term deposits maintained for one to five years. Short-term deposits with less than one-year maturity were withdrawn starting October 1999. In 2005, the maximum maturity period under FCNR(B) deposits was extended to five years and two more currencies (the Canadian dollar and the Australian dollar) were introduced in addition to the existing currencies of U.S. dollar, euro, pound sterling, and yen.

Nonresident (External) Rupee Account (NR(E)RA). The types of NR(E)RA accounts maintained under this include saving, current, or fixed deposits that are repatriable and interest earned thereon is tax exempt. The maturity period for NR(E)RA term deposits is in the range of one to three years. The NR(E)RA account balances are maintained in Indian rupees and thus are exposed to exchange rate risks.

Nonresident Ordinary (NRO) Account. The types of NRO accounts maintained under this include savings, current, or fixed deposits. Current income on these accounts is fully repatriable, as are balances in the account up to US$1 million for bona fide purposes. Interest earned on these accounts is nontax exempt. Upon his/her NRI status, the existing accounts of any Indian national can be designated as an NRO account. Moreover, these accounts can be opened with initial deposits paid into any bank or post office (savings account) authorized to open nonresident accounts. The NRO account gives one the privilege of depositing both overseas as well as Indian earnings.

After reducing the ceiling interest rate on NR(E)RA and FCNR(B) deposits twice in 2007, the RBI increased the rate three times since September 2008 mainly to contain the volatility in the capital flows caused by liquidity constraints in the overseas market. In response to the increased interest rate ceilings, NRI deposits significantly jumped from a low of US$38.8 billion at the end of October 2008 to US$47.4 billion at the end of January 2010 (see figure 2.5) (RBI 2010b).

Part of India's remittance boom is an increase in withdrawals. As can be seen in figure 2.6, although total remittances have increased by 281 percent since 1999–2000, inward remittances have increased by less (221 percent). Local withdrawals from NRI deposit accounts have recorded a growth of more than 400 percent for the same period. At times, such as in 2001–02, 2003–04, and 2005–06, local withdrawals have exceeded inward remittances.

Impact of the Global Financial Crisis on Remittance Flows to India

Remittances to India slightly declined to US$49.2 billion in calendar year 2009, compared with US$49.9 billion in 2008. Beginning in the second half of 2008, these flows started slowing down because of the global financial crisis. Remittance inflows (measured as private transfers) grew at a rate of nearly 60 percent in the first quarter of 2008 and by 48 percent and 43 percent during the second and third quarters of 2008, respectively, compared with the same periods in the previous year. During the fourth quarter of 2008 and the first quarter of 2009, however, these flows declined by 4.5 percent and 31.5 percent, respectively, compared with the same periods in the previous year (see figure 2.7). Overall, in the first half of 2009 (January–June) remittances declined by 15 percent, from US$26.7 billion to US$23.1 billion, during the same period in 2008. However, as can be seen in figure 2.7, these flows picked up again registering a growth of 5 percent and 4 percent, respectively, in both the second and third quarters of 2009 over the same period in 2008. Therefore, it seems that remittance flows to India declined because of the global financial crisis in only two quarters (last quarter of 2008 and first quarter of 2009).

With the financial crisis and ensuing slowdown hitting many remittance source countries, NRIs, faced with income and employment difficulties, might have substituted remittances to their families by drawing

Figure 2.5 NRI Deposits (inclusive of interest accrued)

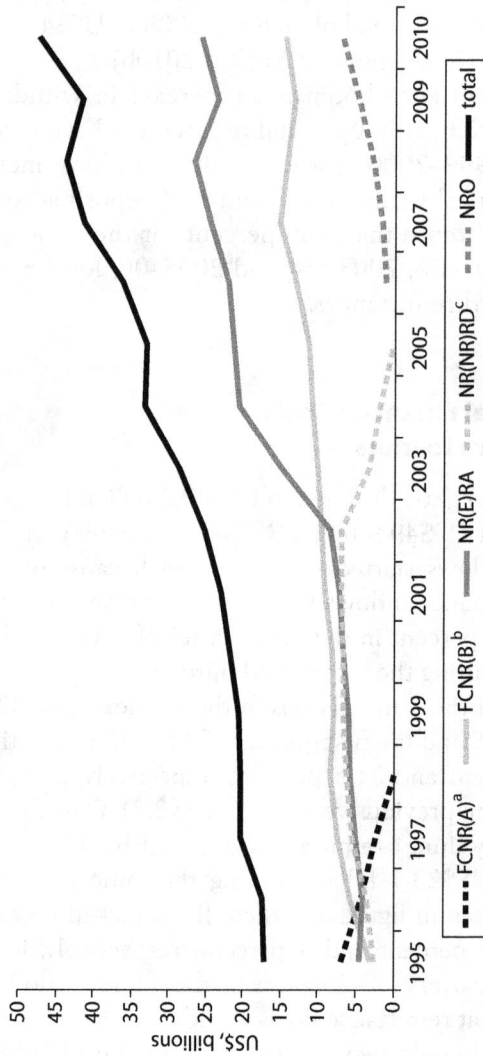

Source: RBI 2010b.

Notes: All data are for end-March, except for 2010 data, which are for end-January.

FCNR(A) = Foreign Currency Nonresident (Accounts); FCNR(B) = Foreign Currency Nonresident—Bank; NR(E)RA = Nonresident (External) Rupee Account; NR(NR)RD = Nonresident (Nonrepatriable) Rupee Deposits; NRO Account = Nonresident Ordinary Account.

a. Withdrawn effective August 1994.

b. Introduced in May 1993.

c. Introduced in 1992 and discontinued in April 2002.

Figure 2.6   Remittances and Local Withdrawals of NRI Deposits

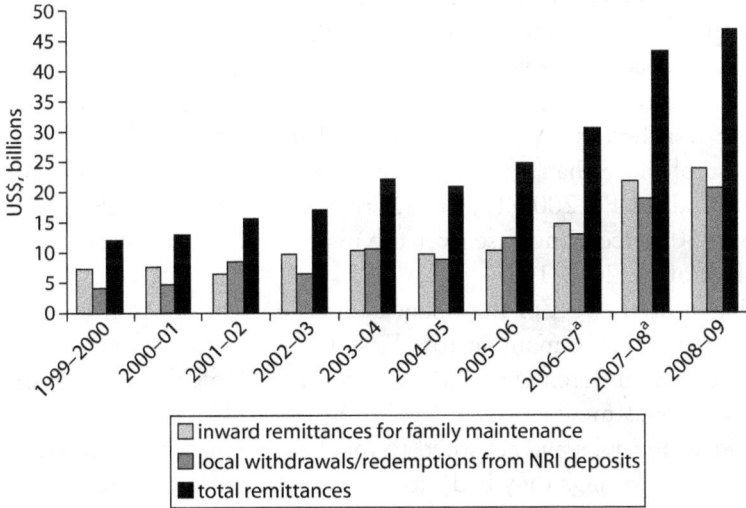

Source: RBI 2010b.
Notes: NRI = Nonresident Indians.
a. = revised.

Figure 2.7   Quarterly Trends in Private Transfers to India

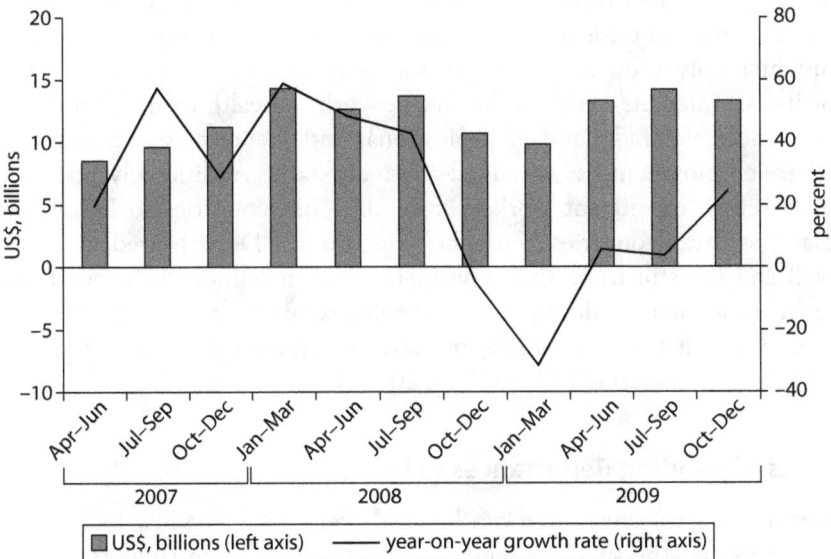

Source: RBI 2010b.

on their foreign currency deposits back in India. Nonresident deposits with Indian banks declined in U.S. dollar terms and in Indian rupees between July and October 2008 (see figure 2.8). This trend, however, started reversing in November 2008, and continues to do so.

Remittance inflows eventually rebounded to US$55 billion in 2010. Private transfers in FY 2009/10 reached more than US$54 billion (an increase of more than 17 percent over the previous fiscal year). For the second half of FY 2009/10, private remittances reached US$30 billion, about a 50 percent increase over the near US$20 billion received in the first half of FY 2009/10.

This limited effect of the financial crisis on remittance flows to India can be attributed to many factors. First, falling asset prices in India, rising interest rate differentials, and a depreciation of the local currency attracted investments from migrants. Second, although some migrants have lost their jobs and returned to India (bringing with them whatever accumulated savings they had), many who have lost jobs are not leaving but rather are taking lower paying jobs with other employers. Other migrants have sent their families home with their accumulated savings to cope with economic uncertainty. Third, even though the overall employment in the high-income countries has declined, the employment prospects for Indian migrants in those countries remained relatively stable during the crisis (Mohapatra and Ratha 2009).

This stable employment is the result of the sectors they are engaged in. The financial crisis mostly hit the construction and real estate sectors in which only a few Indian migrants are employed. A significant number of Indian migrants, on the other hand, work in health care and retail or the wholesale trade, and in professional and technical services sectors where employment has remained relatively stable. Additionally, no large-scale return of migrant workers from the Gulf countries to India took place, as these countries (with the exception of Dubai) fared the crisis well and are still using their considerable oil revenues to finance long-term infrastructure development. Finally, remittance flows tend to be more resilient when the migration destinations are diverse, as is the case with Indian migration (World Bank 2010a).

Costs of Sending Remittances to India

Remittances transfers often can be costly relative to the low incomes of remitters and the small amounts involved, especially in rural areas. The costs of sending money vary and are influenced by several factors, such as

Figure 2.8   Monthly Trends in Nonresident Deposits to India

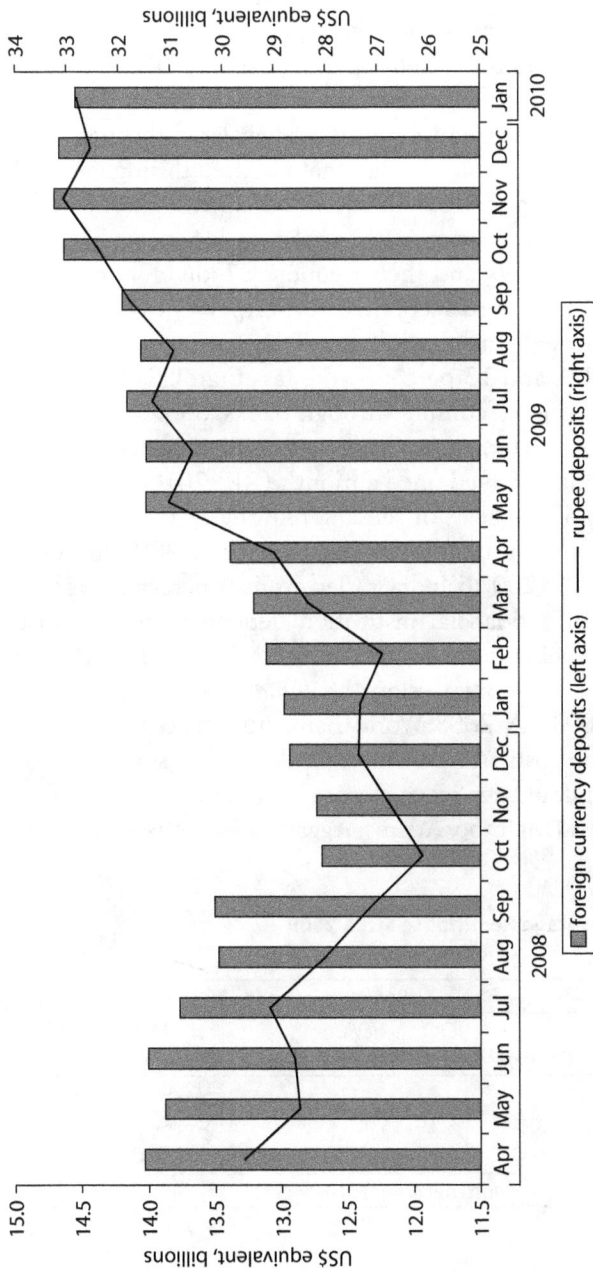

US$ equivalent, billions (left axis)

US$ equivalent, billions (right axis)

■ foreign currency deposits (left axis)   —— rupee deposits (right axis)

Source: RBI 2010b.

destination, transfer method, payments infrastructure, awareness and education levels of migrants, income levels, extent of market competition, and the prevailing rules and regulations.

Remittance transfers to India using banking channels tend to be larger and less frequent than those using Money Transfer Operators (MTOs). In general the ticket size of a remittance initiated through a bank-operated service is two-times higher than that initiated through an MTO (see table 2.3). This corresponds to the findings of an RBI survey of banks in 2009, which also found that an inverse relationship exists between the size of remittance transfers and their frequency. Individual remittance transfers of US$1,100 or more accounted for 42 percent of the total remittance transfers through banks, while around 40 percent were for amounts less than US$500, and 15 percent were less than US$110 in value. Of total remittance inflows coming through banks, 65 percent were received at least once a quarter, with 13 percent being received once a year, and 42 percent being received once a month (RBI 2010a).

In terms of the costs of sending remittance transfer to India, an Inter-American Development Bank (IADB) study in 2003 showed that the cost of sending US$200 to India varied from 6 percent to 14 percent when sent through a financial institution depending on the institution type (with banks being more expensive than MTOs). The study found that the cost of sending money using the *hundi* was much less at 2.5 percent (Orozco 2003). A 2005 World Bank study and field survey found that although the costs of remitting to India have been declining, households in recipient countries receive more local currency when unofficial channels are used (Maimbo, Adams, Aggarwal, and Passas 2005).

Table 2.3   Average Remittance Sizes, 2009
U.S. dollars

| | Banks | | | | | Money Transfer Operators (MTO) | | | |
	Citibank	ICICI bank	HDFC bank	Axis	SBI	WU/ HDFC	Wall Street Forex	WU	UAE Ex.
Average Remittance Size	2,000–3,000	1,500–2,000	5,000–10,000	1,600–2,000	1,000	500–700	400–500	500	350–450

	Internet (Times of Money)	India Post
Average Remittance Size	2,000	70

Sources: Industry sources; authors' interviews and survey.
Note: SBI = State Bank of India; UAE Ex. = UAE Exchange; WU = Western Union.

The RBI 2010 study found an inverse relationship between the speed and the cost of remittance transfers to India through banks. Around 63 percent of remittances to India were transferred through commercial banks by electronic wire/Society for Worldwide Interbank Financial Telecommunications (SWIFT). Although very fast as a form of transfer (one to three days), charges for electronic wire transfers by banks can be high (the cost of sending up to US$500 is 0.2–5 percent and for sending amounts between US$500 and US$1,000 is 0.2–2.5 percent). Checks and drafts can cost less (the cost of sending up to US$500 is less than 2 percent and for sending amounts between US$500 and US$1,000 is less than or equal to 1 percent), but they can take up to 30 days to transfer funds (RBI 2010a). These findings were similar to the findings of a previous RBI study in 2006, although they showed a decrease in the costs of sending money to India, primarily for lower-value transactions (RBI 2006). Both studies estimated that the handling charges imposed domestically on rerouting funds to deliver to noncustomers or remote locations were in the range of 0.1–0.6 percent of the remitted funds. These were additional charges to those paid by the sender of the funds.

A World Bank 2009 field survey of RSPs found that prices of remittance transfers to India differ depending on (among others) three main variables: sending country, remittance-sending scheme (explained in detail in chapter 3), and type of RSP. Prices were in the range of US$0–5 (plus a foreign exchange [FX] fee in the range of 1 to 2 percent) for remittances from GCC countries using *bank-led schemes* and US$5–10 (plus the FX fee of 2 to 5 percent) for remittances from most countries using MTOs. As for Internet money transfer services for remittances from Canada, Singapore, the United Kingdom, and the United States, prices ranged from US$0–5 (plus the FX fee of 1–3 percent).

The World Bank's Global Remittance Price database (World Bank 2010b) provides estimates for the cost of sending remittances to India from various sending countries, for a representative set of RSPs. The database was launched in 2008 and estimates the costs of sending remittances in more than 120 corridors. Table 2.4 represents the costs of sending remittances (US$200 or US$500) to India from important remittance corridors in the first quarter of 2010. The table reports average costs, as well as the maximum and minimum costs paid for using both MTOs and banks to transfer money to India. As seen in the table, for all segments, the percentage cost of sending remittances declines as the amount sent increases. Costs of sending remittances to India are the lowest from Saudi Arabia, Singapore, and the United Arab Emirates, and they are the highest from Canada. For the United Kingdom, banks are

Table 2.4   Costs of Sending Remittances to India, 2009

Source country	Average cost of remitting US$200		Minimum cost of remitting US$200		Maximum cost of remitting US$200		Average cost of remitting US$500		Minimum cost of remitting US$500		Maximum cost of remitting US$500	
	%	US$	%	US$	%	US$	%	US$	%	US$	%	US$
Canada												
Banks	10.3	20.7	4.4	8.7	20.1	40.1	6.9	34.6	3.0	14.9	15.9	79.4
MTOs	7.3	14.6	5.6	11.2	9.1	18.2	4.5	22.5	2.8	14.1	5.8	28.8
Total average	9.5	18.9					6.2	31.0				
Saudi Arabia												
Banks	5.1	10.3	4.4	8.8	5.8	11.7	3.1	15.3	2.4	12.0	3.6	17.9
MTOs	4.7	9.5	3.1	6.3	5.8	11.7	2.7	13.6	1.9	9.7	3.6	17.9
Total average	4.9	9.8					2.9	14.3				
Singapore												
Banks	6.1	12.2	3.1	6.2	11.0	21.9	3.8	19.1	2.6	13.0	5.8	29.0
MTOs	3.9	7.8	2.9	5.8	5.5	11.0	3.3	16.4	2.8	14.2	3.9	19.3
Total average	5.0	10.0					3.5	17.7				
United Arab Emirates												
Banks	26.0	51.9	22.6	45.1	29.4	58.7	11.7	58.4	10.3	51.6	13.0	65.2
MTOs	2.7	5.4	1.4	2.8	4.2	8.4	1.6	7.8	1.0	5.0	2.6	12.8
Total average	4.9	9.8					2.5	12.7				
United Kingdom												
Banks	3.9	7.8	1.3	2.6	5.5	10.9	2.2	10.9	1.3	6.5	3.0	14.8
MTOs	6.2	12.3	2.6	5.2	10.2	20.4	4.1	20.3	2.5	12.3	6.5	32.3
Total average	5.4	10.8					3.4	17.2				
United States												
Banks	8.4	16.7	1.2	2.4	15.0	30.0	5.5	27.3	1.2	6.0	10.8	54.0
MTOs	5.9	11.7	2.3	4.7	8.4	16.9	3.5	17.7	1.6	7.9	6.7	33.7
Total average	7.0	13.9					4.4	21.9				

Source: World Bank 2010b.
Note: MTO = Money Transfer Operator.

less costly channels than MTOs, whereas the reverse is true for Saudi Arabia, Singapore, and the United Arab Emirates.[6] In the case of Canada and the United States, the cost of sending remittances to India can be cheaper using certain banks than using MTOs, although, on average, banks are slightly more expensive.

The Global Remittance Price database (World Bank 2010b) also allows for comparison between costs of sending remittances for 2008, the first and third quarters of 2009, and for the first quarter of 2010 (see figure 2.9). The cost of sending remittances has declined consistently over time only for sending US$200 from Canada. In all other corridors and for both

Figure 2.9   Trend in Total Average Cost of Remitting US$200 and US$500, Q1 2010

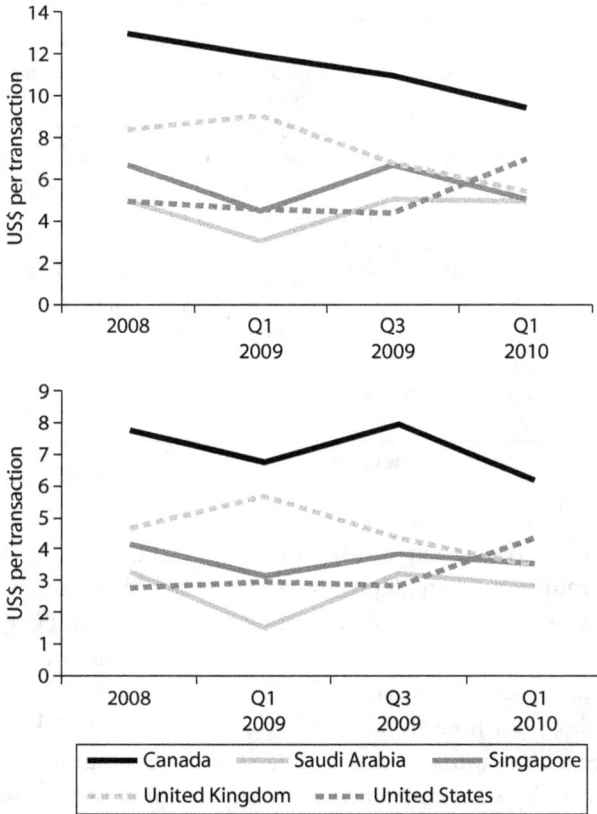

Source: World Bank 2010b.

US$200 and US$500, no consistent pattern can be observed, except for a declining trend in the United Kingdom. The cost of sending remittances from the United States went up drastically for both remittance amounts in the first quarter of 2010. Interestingly, the cost of sending US$200 and US$500 from Saudi Arabia and Singapore to India experienced a sharp decline in the first quarter of 2009 but went back to trend afterward.

Leveraging Remittance Flows for Financial Access in India

Provision of remittances through banking channels can expand financial inclusion in a number of ways (see table 2.5). Remittances can act as a catalyst for individuals to start a relationship with a financial institution

Table 2.5   Development Potential of Remittances-Linked Financial Products

Class of product	Development potential
Remittance transfer services	• Innovative services increase remittances and create a savings culture • Lower costs and increased convenience incentivizes remittances • Remittances can be bundled with other products
Savings	• Savings help in risk mitigation and investment opportunities • Formal savings products are secure and earn interest • Savings accounts provide reliable funds for banks to lend to businesses
Credit	• Credit can be used for consumption as well as for investment needs • Remittances can be used as collateral
Insurance	• Insurance facilitates the management of risks related to health or belongings in which the remittance sender and receiver have a common interest • Insurance can protect entrepreneurs against inhibitive risks in business
Other	• Credit cards and checking accounts that are linked to remittances may facilitate entrepreneurs' purchase of collateral or the management of cash flow

Source: Based on Comstock, Iannone, and Bhatia 2009.

and, in turn, build a credit history. Banks are able to make more loans when more remittances are deposited with them. Moreover, by using bank accounts with regular payment receipts, remittance recipients can access other financial products and services, which typically are not provided by other remittance service providers. With access to savings, insurance, and credit facilities, poor households can better manage their risks. Banks thus are able to reach the unbanked and underserved population and to expand financial access by offering remittance services. In countries with underdeveloped financial sectors, remittances provided through banking channels can alleviate credit constraints for the poor and promote growth.

According to a World Bank survey (2006), most remittance-receiving households in India reported receiving these remittances in cash. Among those households reporting receipt of remittances, 82 percent reported cash as their main mode of remittances, followed by about 15 percent reporting checks or drafts, and close to 2 percent reporting postal money orders. Market assessment for financial services by recipients of international remittance transfers (conducted by MicroSave, India, [Pande and Shukla 2009]) show that remittance recipients value financial services linked to remittances, such as the cash on credit service offered by couriers as an advance against future remittances.

According to Indian RSPs,[7] the main instruments used by migrants to send remittances to India include electronic wire transfers, drafts, checks, money orders, and prepaid credit or debit cards. Most RSPs are serving urban areas and their rural penetration is limited. Their lending technology is inadequate to reach the clientele that microfinance institutions (MFIs) and business correspondents (BCs) can serve more effectively. Currently, the majority of the remittances received through the banks are originated as account-to-account transfers and the rest as cash-to-account transfers and cash-to-cash transfers. For those who do not have accounts with the institutions, identification documents (passport, driver's license, voter card, Permanent Account Number [PAN] card) and proof of residence or utility bill are required to receive remittances. The use of information communications technology (ICT) in providing remittance services is widely prevalent (Internet, automated teller machines [ATMs], and smart cards).

RSPs in India recognize the market potential for innovative financial products linked to remittances. However, they emphasize the lack of indepth analysis of the financial needs of such clientele to develop appropriate financial products for them. In addition, MFIs, which have extensive outreach especially in underbanked areas, are not allowed to offer international remittance services. In addition, India Post has not been able to leverage its large network to provide efficient remittance services or to link these services to its financial products mainly because of inadequate IT infrastructure and operational arrangements. Currently, the remittance-related financial product offerings in India are limited to the following:

Savings products. The benefits of savings products include their interest-earning potential, security, and opportunity to build credibility and a relationship with a financial institution. Some banks in India are offering special remittance-savings accounts, which include all the features of a regular savings account but have no minimum balance requirements. A few banks also have introduced remittance cards onto which remittances are deposited. These cards, which are targeted at unbanked recipients, then can be used at any ATM for cash payout and also can be used as debit cards. Because of the prevailing Know Your Customer (KYC) norms, banks typically require the recipients to provide an identification document. In addition, a proof of residence and a passport-size photograph also are needed to open savings accounts or remittance card accounts.

Loan products. A regular flow of remittances can be used as a substitute for credit histories or collateral. Currently, Indian banks do not provide any special remittance-linked loan products, although all of these banks have indicated an interest in designing and offering such products. For people who are receiving remittances, using remittance flows as collateral or to build credit history is not feasible. The regular loan products are the only ones available through the banking institutions.

Insurance products. In terms of the insurance products, remittances can be used to pay premiums for life or nonlife insurance products. To some extent, remittances act as a substitute for market-based insurance services. Although the potential market for insurance products is vast, such products are not offered specifically to the remittance recipients. Regulations in India do not allow banks to offer insurance services directly. However, banks can offer insurance services through partnerships with insurance companies and agents.

Financial institutions in India have not yet taken active steps to expand outreach through remittance-linked financial products. From the demand-side perspective, the problem lies with the lack of understanding about the financial service needs of remittance recipients. From the supply-side perspective, the efforts to expand financial access through remittances would come from bringing the unbanked remittance recipients into the financial system by reducing costs, improving the speed of delivery, and designing appropriate products. Indian RSPs are interested in receiving technical assistance to develop such products as well as to learn from international best practices.

Notes

1. These amounts represent officially recorded remittance transfers for each fiscal year (April 1 to March 31).

2. The survey is conducted by the University of Maryland in collaboration with the National Council for Applied Economic Research (NCAER). See http://ihds.umd.edu/index.html for details.

3. Remittance inflows from North American could be overestimated: Indian banks receiving remittance transfers from GCC banks using correspondent banking arrangements through the United States may record the transaction as a remittance transfers from the United States instead of the Gulf countries.

4. Estimated using the assumptions and arguments explained in Ratha and Shaw (2007).

5. Discrepancies between World Bank and RBI estimates originate from the fact that World Bank estimates are model based (derived from Ratha and Shaw [2007] assumptions and arguments) and include both banks and

MTOs, while those from RBI are based on recorded bank inflows for the specified time period and suffer from the data recording issues explained in the previous page.

6. The MTO channel for the GCC countries, Malaysia, and Singapore is not really a cash-to-cash remittance. Although at the sending side the MTO is collecting the remittance, on the Indian side (as per RBI guidelines explained in chapter 3), it typically is an Indian bank that has a partnership with that MTO, which processes the remittance transfer and credits it to the recipient's bank account.

7. A survey and interviews took place in November 2009 with seven top RSPs (in terms of remittance volume), including State Bank of India, ICICI Bank, HDFC Bank, Citibank, Axis Bank, Federal Bank, and Times of Money. They covered various remittance-related topics, such as costs, volume, sources, and remittance-linked financial products. Arguably, these RSPs cover about half the Indian remittance market.

References

Comstock, M., M. Iannone, and R. Bhatia. 2009. "Maximizing the Value of Remittances for Economic Development." Research Paper prepared for Solvay Brussels School, Brussels.

Gupta, P. 2006. "Macroeconomic Determinants of Remittances: Evidence from India." Working Paper 05/224, International Monetary Fund, Washington, DC.

Maimbo, S. R. Adams, R. Aggarwal, and N. Passas. 2005. *Migrant Labor Remittances in South Asia.* Direction in Development Series. Washington, DC: World Bank.

Mohapatra, S., and D. Ratha. 2009. "Impact of Global Financial Crisis on Remittances and Migration in India." World Bank, Washington, DC.

MOIA (Ministry of Overseas Indian Affairs). 2009. *Annual Report 2008–2009.* Available at http://moia.gov.in (accessed October 1, 2009).

Orozco, M. 2003. "Worker Remittances in International Scope." Working Paper commissioned by the Multilateral Investment Fund of the Inter-American Development Bank, Washington DC.

Pande, S., and V. Shukla. 2009. "Exploring Domestic Remittances as a New Line of Business for Indian MFIs." India Focus Note 28. Microsave.

Ratha, D., and W. Shaw. 2007, "South-South Migration and Remittances." Bank Working Paper 102, World Bank, Washington, DC.

RBI (Reserve Bank of India). 2008. "Features of Various Deposit Schemes Available to Non-Resident Indians." *Reserve Bank of India Bulletin,* June 1.

————. 2010a. "Remittances from Overseas Indians: Modes of Transfer, Transaction Cost and Time Taken." *Reserve Bank of India Bulletin*, April 13.

————. 2010b, "NRI Deposits: Outstanding/Inflows and Outflows." *Reserve Bank of India Bulletin*, March 10.

World Bank. 2006. "Improving Access to Finance for India's Rural Poor." Directions in Development Series. Washington, DC: World Bank.

————. 2008. "Migration and Development Brief 10." Development Prospects Group, World Bank, Washington, DC.

————. 2010a. "Migration and Development Brief 12." World Bank, Washington, DC.

————. 2010b. World Bank's Global Remittance Price Database. Available at http://remittanceprices.worldbank.org/ (accessed April 15, 2010).

CHAPTER 3

The Remittance Market in India

This chapter describes the remittance market in India in terms of the players involved, the regulatory framework governing the remittance products, and the different existing operational schemes. The chapter identifies and describes the various players in the market (both the official remittance service providers [RSPs] and the unofficial ones) and then explains the regulatory framework applicable for operating remittance services within the Indian market. Based on this framework, the last section of the chapter describes the different existing operational schemes for the transfer of remittances in which the various RSPs have engaged. The information in this chapter sets the stage for the analysis of the market, which is undertaken in chapter 4 and the resulting recommendations.

The Players

The remittance market in India is serviced by commercial banks, nonbank Money Transfer Operators (MTOs), foreign exchange bureaus, cooperative banks, and post offices, as well as a wide variety of commercial entities acting as agents (and subagents). In the rest of this report, banks, nonbanking financial institutions, and MTOs operating remittance services in India are collectively referred to as RSPs. Many of these providers enter into commercial arrangements with exchange houses and other entities in the sending countries to source remittances from migrants. In addition to these providers, a range of other arrangements like *hundi* and *hawala* also service the Indian remittance market. The remittances processed by these arrangements are not recorded and are considered illegal as per the current legal provisions governing remittances.

Estimated Market Share of Remittance Service Providers in India
Banks have the highest share in the remittance market in India. Because of the limited availability of reliable data, it is difficult to estimate the market share of the various RSPs in India. Industry estimates vary, according to ICICI Bank, banks dominate the remittance service market with a 55–60 percent share, money transfer operators account for about 35 percent market share, and Internet RSPs account for the balance (ICICI Bank 2007). Other industry sources claim that as much as 80 percent of recorded remittances flow through the banks and the rest through MTOs.

Banks
Banks are major players in India's remittance market. Both state-owned and private sector banks are taking the lead in the remittance service market by building specific technology platforms to provide remittance services, and they also are entering into partnerships with entities abroad to source remittances. The banking system covers through its branches all the states and the districts in the country, with the branch network covering many rural and semiurban areas as well. According to industry sources, among the banks, currently State Bank of India (SBI) and ICICI Bank dominate the market for remittances with an estimated market share of 25 percent and 20 percent, respectively. They have banking operations in many foreign countries and are leveraging their branch networks abroad to source remittances. Banks primarily process remittances that are credited to the recipient's account. Many banks also offer remittances services as agents of MTOs, wherein they disburse cash to the recipient from their branches.

The interbank infrastructure composed of Real-Time Gross Settlement (RTGS) and National Electronic Funds Transfer (NEFT) systems are being used for remittances. These systems have played a big role in reducing the remittance processing time and also have enabled MTOs to move funds faster to their agents.

Money Transfer Operators

MTOs such as Western Union (WU), MoneyGram, and others are the second most widely used RSPs in India. MTOs operate in India through alliances, partnerships, and subagencies. Many banks have entered into partnerships with these MTOs and act as their principal agent. WU is the leader in this segment; it has more than 50,000 agent locations in India, operates in more than 7,000 cities and towns, and works with more than 30 leading banks. India Post is among the largest agents of WU. The services of MTOs are believed to be convenient and reliable. MTOs process primarily remittances that are paid out in cash to the recipients.

India Post

Beginning in early 2000, India Post started offering various remittance-related facilities, such as international money transfers, and it partnered with WU to support the transfer of funds into India using the post office network. India Post with its large network of branches across the country provides a trusted and easy-to-access outlet for financial services, such as savings,[1] insurance, and money order services.

India Post has its own remittance product offerings, namely, a money order (MO) service and a postal order (PO) service. These instruments enable sending money using the postal network of around 160,000 post offices. An MO is a cash-to-cash service used for domestic remittances: the originating post office collects the full amount of the payment, plus a commission, from the person sending the funds and sends an advice to the destination post office, where the funds are paid to the beneficiary, either at the post office or by a postal worker at the doorstep of the beneficiary. A gap of 5–10 days usually exists between the sender initiating the MO and the beneficiary receiving the funds. Around 2,000 post offices offer instant MOs for transfer. POs are paper-based instruments akin to a demand draft. The sender pays the funds at a post office and receives the PO, which he or she can send to the beneficiary. The beneficiary can present this PO at any post office and will receive funds after they are cleared through the postal network. The post office is a principal agent of WU, under an exclusivity agreement. Around 8,500 post offices offer WU services.

Internet

With the use of technology becoming increasingly popular among financial service providers, Internet-based provision of remittance services has become a fast-growing business. Advancement in communications technology has made the business of international payments fast, flexible, and relatively less costly. The process is simple and paper free, and it helps the remitter track the processing of the remittance.

Private banks such as HDFC and ICICI have started offering Internet-based remittance services. Among state-owned banks, SBI and Bank of India have introduced online remittance services: e-remit and star-e-remit, respectively. Times of Money, a nonbanking company, also has been active in this business through its Remit2India website (see box 3.1).

Other Channels

As in other South Asian countries, community-based arrangements for remittance transfers also are used in India. These arrangements include courier transfers, in-kind remittances, and *hawala/hundi*. The characteristics of *hawala* money transfers (predominantly used in the Middle East and South Asia) include ease of operation, lower transaction costs, speed, potential anonymity, and convenience, which explain their usage even today.

Box 3.1

Remit2India

Remit2India, a part of the Times of India group, provides an Internet-based money transfer service to India. Currently, this service is available for Nonresident Indians (NRIs) in 23 countries.

To send remittances through Remit2India, the remitter has to register with Remit2India and to give them online instructions to transfer money.[a] The specified amount then is deducted from the remitter's bank account abroad and is transferred using Remit2india to the requested bank account or person in India. Currently, money can be remitted in nine currencies through this service. The remittance can be sent directly to an Indian bank account or, if the remitter opts for a demand draft facility, the remittance is door delivered as a locally payable demand draft in Indian rupees. The average processing time is three to five days but can be further decreased if higher priced express delivery service is used. Recipients also can choose to receive a prepaid card; the remittance amount is loaded onto the card. The card can then be used at ATMs and point-of-sale (POS) terminals.

Source: http://www.remit2india.tv/index.html.
Note: a. The money can be transferred using various options, including check, wire, PayPal, credit card, rupee express, or money bookers.

In comparison to the courier transfer, which is less efficient and more risky because of the physical transfer of cash across borders, the *hawala* system is more trusted and highly efficient. Although the exact amount of remittances transferred though the *hawala* system is difficult to measure because of its unrecorded nature, some studies estimate that the *hawala* market in India could be as large as 30 to 40 percent of the recorded remittance transfers.

A typical *hawala* transaction consists of a remitter, a recipient, and two intermediaries, that is, *hawaladars*. When transferring the funds to the home country, the migrant–remitter makes payment to an intermediary-*hawaladar* in the remitting country. The *hawaladar* then contacts their partner service provider in the recipient country who then arranges for the payment in local currency to the beneficiary. The beneficiary is required to present a preagreed identification document or code. When this transaction is conducted, the agent in the remitting country is indebted to the agent in the recipient country. Their transactions are settled through similar transactions going in the opposite direction, cash payments, or bank account transfers. In some cases, their positions also can be transferred to other intermediaries.

Regulatory Environment

All foreign exchange (FX) transactions conducted by Indian entities need to conform to the Foreign Exchange Management Act (FEMA) of 1999. FEMA was enacted for the purpose of promoting the development and maintenance of a foreign exchange market in India. FEMA empowers the RBI to regulate, among other things, foreign currency payments into and out of India, including remittances, when either one of the parties to the transaction is located in India. FEMA requires business entities wishing to offer foreign currency–related services to obtain a license under any one of four specific licensing categories called Authorized Dealers (ADs) I to III and Full-Fledged Money Changers (FFMCs). These categories are as follows:

- *Foreign exchange dealers:* These are banks licensed by RBI and allowed to offer all foreign exchange–related services (both current and capital account transactions), including processing and disbursement of international remittances. Licensing category: AD I.
- *Money transfer agents and foreign exchange companies:* These agents are allowed to operate inward and outward remittances, and can undertake the purchase of foreign exchange and sale or remittance of foreign

exchange for specified nontrade current account transactions. Licensing category: AD II

- *Specialized financial institutions:* These institutions include export and import companies and other similar institutions, and can provide foreign exchange services for designated activities like foreign trade. They can undertake transactions incidental to the foreign exchange activities undertaken by these institutions. Licensing category: AD III
- *Full-Fledged Money Changers:* FFMCs are allowed to purchase foreign exchange currency, resell limited amounts of this currency (for Indians traveling abroad), and manage inward remittance business. Licensing category: FFMC.

The licensing criteria for AD II include capital requirements, governance, adequate internal control mechanisms, and regulatory or prudential comfort. ADs are subject to regular oversight and supervision by the Foreign Exchange (FX) Department of the RBI and are required to submit monthly or quarterly information about volumes and value and for certain transactions, including the details of individual transactions. Moreover, the ADs are subject to strong suspect transaction reporting requirements in line with the Anti-Money Laundering (AML)/Combating the Financing of Terrorism (CFT) legislation. Since June 2009, institutions authorized as payment system operators have been included as reporting agencies in accordance with AML/CFT regulations.

Apart from banks (AD I), only entities having an AD II or FFMC license can offer remittance services directly. All these entities are required to seek express approval from the FX Department of RBI to offer these services. The FX Department has created two approval regimes to administer the approval process for remittance services, namely, the Rupee Drawing Arrangement (RDA) and Money Transfer Service Scheme (MTSS).

Remittance services are considered a permitted banking activity; hence banks have general permission to provide remittance services. The general permission, however, allows only the conduct of remittance business in partnership with other domestic banks or with banks in sending countries. Banks in India offering remittance services in partnership with nonbanks in the sending countries need approval from RBI under the RDA.

As for nonbanking entities licensed under AD II or FFMC, they need to offer remittance services in conformity with the MTSS (which is also open to banks or ADs I), and they need express approval from the FX Department of RBI. The entities licensed under the MTSS typically offer remittance services in partnership with international MTOs like WU, MoneyGram, or other foreign MTOs. They also can engage other entities as subagents for disbursement of remittances. In addition, many banks in India (as ADs I or II) have partnered with MTOs to offer remittances services under the MTSS.

The key elements of the RDA are as follows:

- Foreign entities should be regulated by a competent authority in the sending country, and have necessary licenses in the sending country.
- Service should be provided only from Gulf Cooperation Council (GCC)[2] countries; Hong Kong SAR, China; Malaysia; and Singapore.
- No limit on remittance amount.
- A domestic Indian bank can have a maximum of 20 such tie-ups.
- Foreign entity should maintain a Rupee Vostro account with the domestic bank.
- The recipient should be paid only with funds available in the Rupee Vostro account. If funds are not available, the recipient should not be credited.
- The domestic bank needs to ensure that the transactions are compliant to AML and Financial Action Task Force (FATF) guidelines.
- This arrangement can be used for trade-related remittances and remittances for personal or family expenses.

The key aspects of the MTSS are as follows:

- The principal agent should have an authorization provided under FEMA.
- The remittance service should be used only for remittances for family or personal expenses in India.
- One recipient can receive a maximum of US$2,500 per remittance, and can receive only 12 remittances in a calendar year.
- Payouts up to Rs 50,000 can be made in cash, beyond which a check or demand draft is needed.
- The principal agent is responsible for all AML and Know-Your-Customer (KYC) requirements at its own outlets and its subagents.
- The principal agent should maintain a collateral equal to three days' worth of pipeline transactions or US$50,000, whichever is higher. The collateral up to US$50,000 should be in the form of a fixed deposit in a commercial bank, higher amounts can be in the form of a Letter of Credit.

- The principal agent should report the volume data of its entire network on a quarterly basis to the regional RBI office.
- The principal agent should report its list of agents to RBI on a half-yearly basis.
- No capital requirement is prescribed for Indian agents. However, ADs I, ADs II, and FFMCs (which can become Indian agents under MTSS) are required to fulfill minimum capital requirements for their respective AD categories. The minimum capital requirement for subagents is Rs 500,000.
- The principal agent and its network are subject to audit by the RBI unit that supervises its main line of business. For example, for banks, it would be the Department of Banking Supervision, and for rural banks, it would be the National Bank for Agriculture and Rural Development (NABARD), and so on.

The key aspects of these two regimes are summarized in table 3.1.

The Prevalent Operational Schemes

Based on the regulatory framework and the two approval regimes, commercial banks, ADs, and FFMCs in India have created five distinct operational schemes for remittance services. These schemes are described below.

Bank-Operated Scheme: RDA

The RDA bank-operated scheme involves a partnership between an India-based AD I (typically a bank, called here bank partner) and a non-bank company (foreign partner) in the sending country. This scheme operates under the RDA approval regime. The bank is responsible for the disbursement of the remittance to the recipient, and the foreign partner is responsible for the sourcing of funds from the sender. The foreign partner is required to maintain a rupee-denominated account with the bank partner. The bank partner can use only the funds available in this account to disburse funds to the recipients.

Senders can initiate a remittance through various channels, including websites, walking into the branch of a foreign partner in the sending country, phone banking, and so on. The sender pays the remittance amount and fees through available payment instruments in the sending country. In general, the payment mode is cash. For payments made by other instruments, the remittance transaction is kept pending until the

Table 3.1 Comparison of Two Approval Regimes

Criteria	RDA	MTSS
Business arrangement	A bank in India ties up with a nonbank financial services companies in specified countries abroad. The foreign nonbank entity sources the funds from the remitter; the Indian bank disburses the funds in India using its branch network and other interbank payment instruments.	A foreign nonbank/banking services company ties up with banks and nonbanking companies in India, appointing them as principal agents. These principal agents in turn appoint subagents. The foreign partner sources the funds from the remitter; the recipient can collects funds in cash from a conveniently located agent/subagent. The recipient has the choice of receiving payment using other interbank payment instruments.
Who has to apply	The bank in India needs to apply to the Foreign Exchange Department of RBI for approval.	The principal agent in India needs to apply to the Foreign Exchange department of RBI for approval. The foreign partner is termed as the "Overseas Principal" and needs to apply to the Payment and Settlements Department of the RBI for a license, under the Payments and Settlement Systems Act. The principal agent should be AD I, AD II, or FFMC. The eligibility requirement is described further in the subsequent sections. The overseas principal takes one common license. The principal agent needs to take approval for each overseas principal tie-up. The subagents do not need any approval from RBI.
Source countries	Gulf Cooperation Council (GCC) countries, Singapore, and Hong Kong SAR, China. Essentially the countries where RBI has determined that nonbanking financial services companies are regulated effectively by the local monetary authority.	No country-based restriction.
Remittance amount limits	No limit on workers' remittances. A limit of Rs 2 Lakh per remittance on trade remittances exists. Remittance transfer can be for any reason, including for business transactions.	Maximum per remittance limited to US$2,500, with a maximum of 12 remittances per recipient in a calendar year. Remittance is limited for personal use and for family maintenance, remittances for business transactions is expressly prohibited.

(continued next page)

47

Table 3.1 *(continued)*

Criteria	RDA	MTSS
Payout modes	Any interbank payment instrument (but no cash is permitted under RDA).	Cash or any other interbank payment instrument. Amount above Rs 50,000 has to be paid using a noncash payment instrument.
Foreign partner	Only banks or financial institutions that are regulated by the monetary authority of the sending country.	No restriction on the type of entity that can be an overseas principal, however these entities need RBIs approval prior to starting service. During the approval process, RBI applies certain minimum requirements.
Capital and guarantee requirements	The necessary collateral guarantee requirement is prescribed under various scheme of RDA by RBI.	Foreign partner has to place collateral of US$50,000 or three days' average worth of remittances, whichever is higher. The collateral of US$50,000 can be as a fixed deposit in a commercial bank; amounts greater than US$50,000 can be in the form of a letter of credit.
Partnership restrictions	No restrictions	No restrictions
Appointment of agents	Not applicable	Capital requirement specified at the time of approval. Minimum capital Rs 500,000.
AML and KYC requirements	Treated as a standard banking transaction; by default the AML and KYC requirements apply.	The Prevention of Money Laundering Act requires adherence to AML/CFT requirements and specifies KYC requirements.
Reporting requirements	Indian Agents under RDA are required to submit quarterly statements on remittances received to the RBI.	Quarterly reporting of transaction volume and new sub-agent additions.

Source: Author's compilation.

Note: AD = Authorized Dealer; AML = Anti-Money Laundering; CFT = Combating the Financing of Terrorism; FFMC = Full-Fledged Money Changer; KYC = Know Your Customer; RBI = Reserve Bank of India.

payment instrument is cleared and settled through the payment systems in the sending country. The foreign partner informs the sender of the exchange rate for the local currency to Indian rupees, which usually is at a 1–2 percent margin over the interbank rate. The foreign partner also charges a fee to the sender for the remittance, which usually range from US$0–US$5.

At periodic intervals, typically two to three times a day, the foreign partner consolidates all the accepted remittance instructions and transmits the remittance instructions to the bank, using proprietary custom-built interfaces. The corresponding amount in foreign currency is credited to a Nostro account of the bank partner maintained in the sending country or in the United States, with instructions to onward remit that amount to the rupee-denominated account of the foreign partner maintained with the bank partner. In cases in which the bank partner has a branch in the sending country, the Nostro account typically is maintained at that branch. The exchange rate between the foreign currency and Indian rupee is specified by the bank partner. The rupee amount credited to the account of the foreign partner should be equivalent to the rupee amount to be disbursed to the recipients by the bank partner.

The bank partner processes these instructions and credits the recipient's account. If the recipient account is at a different domestic bank, then the recipient is credited through RTGS or NEFT (the interbank electronic funds transfer mechanisms available in India) or through dispatch of a demand draft. In cases in which a demand draft is issued, the recipient is charged a fee. Some banks charge for RTGS or NEFT credits, which usually range from US$1 to US$5. The revenue source for the foreign partner is the difference between the exchange rate offered to the sender and the exchange rate offered by the bank partner, and a portion of the fees charged to the sender. The revenue source of the bank partner is the foreign exchange margins on the conversion to Indian rupees and its share of the fees.

Bank-Operated Scheme: Tie-up with Foreign Bank

This scheme essentially involves a domestic bank entering into agreements with a set of banks (partner bank) in the sending country(s). The domestic bank builds a remittance product around this arrangement and markets this product to senders. Senders can use various channels to initiate the remittance, including websites, walking into the branch of a partner bank, phone banking, and so on, with the source funds being provided through available payment instruments in the sending country.

Because this is a service offered by a domestic bank in partnership with a bank in the sending country, no express permission is required from the RBI. The foreign bank, in general, maintains a rupee-denominated account with the domestic bank. The funds collected from the senders are credited into this account periodically, usually multiple times a day. The operational features of this scheme are identical to the bank-operated RDA scheme. The revenue stream for the bank is the exchange rate margin and its share of the fee charged to the sender.

Internet-Based Remittance Services

Some Indian banks have developed branded online services for remittances, especially in Singapore, the United Kingdom, and the United States. This involves the sender registering for the online service, and providing a debit authorization for debiting his or her account at a local bank in the sending country for onward transfer to a recipient account in India. The Indian bank offering this service utilizes the services of a partner bank in the sending country to clear the debit authorization in the local interbank electronic funds transfer service and then to remit the funds to India. TimesofMoney Limited, a Times Group company, offers a shared platform for operating this service—to date, 18 banks in India have created Internet-based remittance services using this platform. ICICI, SBI, and Federal Bank are operating their own proprietary solutions, with the same broad features.

The domestic bank uses its banking arrangements in the sending country to move the funds collected from the senders to its own books in India. Once the funds are in India, the remittance is credited to the recipient's account, if it is in the same bank, or the NEFT and RTGS infrastructure is used to credit the recipient's account in a different Indian bank. The remittance amount can be credited into the foreign currency–denominated accounts available to NRIs. The revenue stream for the domestic bank is the exchange rate margin and the fees charged to the sender. The costs involved are the operational costs of operating the online service platform.

MTO Service

The most active remittance services operated by MTOs in India include WU, MoneyGram, and the UAE Exchange. These entities (overseas principals) operate through a network of principal agents in the sending country and India. The agent network is typically two-tiered, including principal agents who have a tie-up with the scheme operator, and subagents who are appointed by the principal agent. The principal agents in

India need permission from RBI to operate under the MTSS framework. Leading commercial banks, licensed money changers, and post offices have contracted with international money transfer companies as their principal agents. The licensed money changers, in turn, have appointed other smaller money changers, retail outlets, and reputed commercial entities as their subagents.

This service is typically a fully cash-based mechanism, that is, cash pay-in and cash pay-out. This service works as follows: the sender visits the outlet of the overseas principal or its agents in the sending country; completes a remittance form providing his or her identification details, the contact details of the receiver and a passcode; and deposits the cash. The agent enters the details into a proprietary system provided by the overseas principal and provides a unique transaction number (UTN) to the sender, as well as a list of agent locations where the recipient can receive the remittance. The sender communicates the agent locations, UTN, and passcode to the recipient through offline means (typically a phone call). The recipient visits a convenient agent location; and after due identification using a government-issued photo identification, UTN, and passcode, completes a receipt form and receives the payment in cash. If the receipt amount is more than Rs 50,000, the recipient is provided a check by the agent or is directed to go to a bank agent and receive a check. The agent updates the proprietary system provided by the overseas principal with the payout details. Agents usually display logos of the overseas principal at participating branches, and a recipient can receive the payout at any of these outlets.

The principal agent is reimbursed for the payouts of its agent network by a credit to the agent's Nostro account in a foreign location or to a rupee account. The principal agent then uses this amount to reimburse its subagents. Some large subagents also assist other subagents in the event of cash shortfalls. The overseas principal usually maintains rupee-denominated accounts with a set of banks in India, and issues instructions for payouts to principal agents from this account using RTGS or NEFT. The MTOs have specific risk management and monitoring rules, and they periodically audit the principal agent network and review every subagent appointment. As per market sources, the cost of remittance using this method involves a fixed fee in the range of US$5–10 and an exchange markup of around 3 to 5 percent over the prevailing interbank rates. The revenue source for the MTO is the exchange rate margin and the fee paid by the senders. The revenue source for the principal agent is the per-transaction fee paid by the MTO, which typically is in the range of US$2–5.

Table 3.2 Key Aspects of the Five Remittance Operational Schemes

Attribute	Bank-RDA	Bank tie-up	Internet	MTO	Wire transfer
Approval framework	RDA	No permission required	No permission required	MTSS	No permission required
Indian entity operating the service	AD I (mostly commercial banks)	Commercial bank	Commercial bank	ADs I, ADs II, and FFMCs	Commercial bank
Foreign partner	Exchange house	Bank	No specific partner; usually part of existing service arrangements for banking activities	MTO	No specific partner; usually part of existing service arrangements for banking activities
Pay-in location	Exchange houses at sending country, among others	Bank branch in foreign country or through electronic channels of foreign partner bank	Internet or call center	Exchange house	Bank branch or electronic channels offered by bank
Pay-in modes	Cash or paper instrument	Cash or paper instrument or electronic transfer	Electronic transfer	Cash	Paper instrument or electronic transfer
Pay-out modes	Credit to account or paper instrument mailed to recipient	Credit to account or paper instrument mailed to recipient	Credit to account or paper instrument mailed to recipient	Cash or paper instrument handed over to recipient	Credit to account
Payout locations	Not applicable	Not applicable	Not applicable	Agent location	Not applicable
End-to-end time	Instant to 1 day	1–2 days	3–5 days	Instant	1–3 days
Cost (%)	$0–5 + 1–2	$0–5+1–2	$0–5+1–3	$5–10 + 2–5	$10–30 + 1–2
Countries available	GCC countries, Singapore, and Malaysia	Worldwide, particularly United Kingdom, GCC countries, Singapore, and Malaysia	Worldwide, particularly Canada, United Kingdom, United States, and Singapore	Worldwide	Worldwide

Source: Author's research.

Note: AD = Authorized Dealer; FFMC = Full-Fledged Money Changer; GCC = Gulf Cooperation Council; MTO = Money Transfer Operator; MTSS = Money Transfer Service Scheme; RDA = Rupee Drawing Arrangement.

Wire Transfers

These transfers are the standard Society for Worldwide Interbank Financial Telecommunication (SWIFT)–based, cross-border, credit transfer instructions. They are available to senders who have access to a bank supporting international wire transfers and whose recipient has an account in India, which is allowed to receive incoming foreign exchange transactions. These arrangements usually have a series of correspondent banks involved to link the sending and receiving financial institution. Typically, each foreign correspondent bank would charge between US$5 and US$20 as fees; if a domestic correspondent bank is required to reach the domestic recipient bank, then in general RTGS or NEFT is used, and a fee in the range of Rs 25–200 is applied. The sender has an option to indicate whether the remittance would need to be sent in foreign currency or in Indian rupees. In case the instruction is to remit in foreign currency, and the destination account is denominated in rupees, the recipient bank would apply the prevailing exchange rate and charge a service fee. As per current service tax rules, this fee also attracts a service tax. This instrument is widely used for trade-related settlements, but it is not popular for remittances. In general, the recipient receives funds in his or her bank account within three days depending on the time of initiation, intervening holidays, and so on.

Tables 3.2 and 3.3 summarize and map the key aspects of these five schemes.

Table 3.3   Mapping of Remittance Schemes to Types of Authorized Institutions

Type of institution	Type of scheme				
	RDA scheme	Bank - bank tie-up	MTSS	Internet	Wire transfer
AD I (non-banks)	Yes	No	As principal agent and subagent of MTO	No	No
AD I (banks)	Yes	Yes	As principal agent and subagent of MTO	Yes	Yes
AD II	No	No	As principal agent and subagent of MTO	No	No
AD III	No	No	No	No	No
FFMC	No	No	As principal agent and subagent of MTO	No	No

Source: Authors' research
Note: AD = Authorized Dealer; FFMC = Full-Fledged Money Changer; MTO = Money Transfer Operator; MTSS = Money Transfer Service Scheme.

Notes

1. It is estimated that there are more than 200 million such accounts.
2. The GCC is composed of six countries: Bahrain, Kuwait, Oman, Qatar, Saudi Arabia, and the United Arab Emirates.

Reference

ICICI Bank. 2007. "Global Remittances." Presentation prepared for Asian Bank to Bank Forum, BAFT.

CHAPTER 4

Diagnostic of the Remittance Market in India

This chapter reviews the remittance market in India on the basis of the General Principles for International Remittances (GPs) developed jointly by the Committee on Payment and Settlement Systems and the World Bank (CPSS-WB) and includes several observations for the improvement and future development of the market for the provision of remittance services in India. Some of the observations presented in this chapter already are known to the Indian authorities, and in certain cases, they are considered for action, whereas in other cases, additional insights have been identified. As recognized in the GPs (http://www.bis.org/publ/cpss76.htm), for attempts to improve the market for remittances to be fully effective, actions will need to be taken in both the relevant sending and receiving countries. Several actions can be taken directly in India, however, as highlighted in this chapter.

This chapter is organized as follows: the first five sections focus on the actual application of the GPs. The following two sections deal with the role of market players and public authorities, respectively, in applying these principles, and the last section provides recommendations on improving financial access through remittance-linked products.

Transparency and Consumer Protection: The Market for Remittance Services Should Be Transparent and Have Adequate Consumer Protection (GP 1)

Transparency in remittance services, combined with adequate consumer protection, helps to foster a competitive and safe market for remittances. Transparency of prices and service features is crucial to enable consumers to make informed choices between different services and for the creation of a competitive market. Remittance Service Providers (RSPs) therefore should be encouraged to provide such information in accessible and understandable formats. At a minimum, the information provided should include the total price (that is, fees at both ends, foreign exchange rates, including the margins applied on them, and other costs to the user), the time it will take the funds to reach the receiver, and the specific locations of the RSP's access points in both sending and receiving countries.

Appropriate consumer protection is also important. Senders should have adequate rights as consumers of remittance services, including error-resolution administrative procedures. Although many countries have mechanisms to resolve domestic consumer disputes, the cross-border nature of remittances and cultural and language barriers can make such procedures complex.

Transparency and Consumer Protection in India's Remittance Market

The market for remittances in India appears to be transparent and con-sumers are informed about the different aspects of the transaction. When receiving money through a Money Transfer Operator (MTO), the recipi-ent generally does not pay any charge, whereas when remittances are sent through banks, an additional fee could be charged to credit the recipients' account with a different bank. In general, senders are informed about such a charge. Most MTOs in India operate toll-free customer service numbers, which are operational on all business days during business hours. For bank-operated services, the recipient can access the standard customer service channels of the bank. On the sending side, the RSPs ensure that their partners' service centers in the sending countries display the exchange rates and service charges. The sender is provided a receipt, which clearly states the exchange rate, the service charge, and the amount in Indian rupees that the recipient would receive.

Bank-operated remittance services are subject to the general customer protection and transparency measures specified by the Reserve Bank of

India (RBI) for all banking transactions. The Money Transfer Service Scheme (MTSS), under which the MTOs offer remittance services, does not prescribe any specific customer protection and transparency measures. Still, most RSPs in India, including MTOs, enforce specific customer protection measures: the sender is informed when the recipient receives funds and if he or she does not collect the funds within a specified number of days. Complaints by senders and recipients are addressed in a timely manner. The level of complaints and disputes seems to be low, and reported transaction defaults are at a minimum. In most cases, reported problems are linked primarily to mistakes in the transcription of the recipient's account details and to cash shortages in some disbursing locations.

In case of unresolved issues, bank customers can approach the banking ombudsman; in addition, the usual legal resolutions schemes are available. The latter are the only available recourse for MTOs customers. There have been no reported instances of the legal system being used for resolving remittance-related issues.

Observations and Suggested Actions

The RBI could consider requiring RSPs to adopt robust consumer protection measures. The RSPs in India already have adopted a range of good customer protection measures. To ensure continued adherence to these measures and also to ensure new entrants do not dilute standards, it is recommended that the RBI, as part of the Rupee Drawing Arrangement (RDA) and MTSS approvals require the RSPs to (a) adopt a consumer protection charter, which is widely publicized; and (b) designate grievance handling officers and publicize their contact details (senders and receivers should be encouraged to contact these officers with complaints that have not been addressed through the RSPs standard dispute resolution mechanism). The consumer charter should have a clear description of the service terms and conditions, the rights of the consumer, and the dispute resolution mechanism. The World Bank has developed a draft of a model customer charter, this currently is under review for adoption by the G-8 Remittances Working Group. The text of this draft is available in appendix D of this report. This can be adapted for use in India.

The RBI could consider extending the ombudsman service to cover MTO-operated schemes. Currently, the bank-operated remittance services are covered by the banking ombudsman service. To ensure the same level of customer protection for the MTO scheme, the ombudsman services can be extended to the MTO schemes as well.

Payment System Infrastructure: Improvements to Payment System Infrastructure That Have the Potential to Increase the Efficiency of Remittance Services Should Be Encouraged (GP 2)

Remittance services depend at some stage on the domestic payment infrastructure for settlement (and sometimes also for the transfer of information). RSPs often can make better use of the payment infrastructure through greater standardization of payment instruments, more automation of their processing, and increased interoperability of the associated networks.

Improvements to cross-border payment infrastructure that have the potential to increase the efficiency of remittance services also should be encouraged. Sometimes such improvements and initiatives may be undertaken by the market. Given the diverse nature of the institutions involved and the uncertainty about the scale of future flows and thus whether investment in the link is justified, the authorities, and in particular central banks, may want to play a facilitating role. In some cases, it also may be possible to link directly to the relevant domestic retail payment systems of sending and receiving countries.

The Existing Payments Infrastructure

The payment infrastructure in India is composed of payment systems for large-value and retail payments. The RBI plays a key role in operating India's payment systems, for both high-value and retail payments, and in regulating and overseeing these systems. RBI operates the Real-Time Gross Settlement (RTGS), for interbank payments and for high-value and time-critical customer transactions. RTGS was introduced in 2004. All high-value transactions (above Rs 100,000) are settled through the RTGS system.

The retail payment systems operating in India include both paper-based systems (magnetic ink character recognition [MICR] check clearing, non-MICR check clearing) and electronic systems, namely, the Electronic Clearing Service (ECS) and the National Electronic Funds Transfer (NEFT). The check-based instruments still account for a large part of retail payments. Sixteen clearinghouses for paper-based and electronic clearing in the major metropolitan cities (Chennai, Delhi, Kolkata, and Mumbai) and other large cities in the country are operated or managed by the RBI. The settlement of these systems occurs in the accounts of banks maintained with the RBI. In other places, the clearinghouse is managed by the State Bank of India (SBI) (the country's largest public sector bank) and other public sector banks. These banks also perform the settlement bank function in these centers.

Two electronic funds transfer systems currently operate in the country, namely, the ECS (for credit and debit transfers) and the NEFT (which was introduced in November 2005). As of September 2009, about 60,800 bank branches in India were linked to the NEFT network. NEFT is an electronic fund transfer system that provides a nationwide, secure one-to-one retail funds transfer facility for customers with bank accounts. Payments through NEFT can be settlend the same day or the next day (T+1) for the receiving customer depending on the processing efficiency of the recipient bank. ECS is a retail payment system that facilitates bulk payments (both for debit and credit transfers) and that can be used for collection of payments for loan installments, insurance premiums, dividends, tax refunds, payrolls, and pensions distribution. A large portion of payments still are based on checks and drafts, largely because of customer preferences. RBI intends to improve the efficiency of ECS and expand the geographical coverage of NEFT to increase the usage of the electronic retail payment infrastructure in the country.

Payment cards (both debit and credit cards) have registered large growth in India over the past five years. Some 24.7 million credit and 137 million debit cards were issued as of end-March 2009. The number of automated teller machines (ATMs) and point of sale (POS) terminals deployed in the country also has been growing, with POS covering around 150 cities and ATMs covering more than 500 cities. RBI's subsidiary, the Institute for Development and Research in Banking Technology (IDRBT), set up a national ATM acceptance network called the National Financial Switch (NFS)—the technology support for this is provided by Euronet. Currently, 38 banks are connected to the NFS. In addition, two other multilateral ATM acceptance networks include Cashnet (operated by Euronet worldwide) and Cashtree (operated by Fidelity Information Systems). A few other multilateral ATM networks are operated by a set of banks.

Banks issue credit cards using the brand mark of Visa, MasterCard, or American Express, the majority of which are internationally valid and accepted at all ATMs and merchant locations accepting cards with these brand marks. Most debit cards are issued under the brand mark of Visa or MasterCard; only a few limited proprietary cards are available. Visa- or MasterCard-branded cards in general are valid internationally at ATMs and merchant locations accepting these brands. Proprietary cards are accepted at only the issuing banks' ATMs or the NFS or ATMs of banks with whom the issuing bank has a bilateral or multilateral arrangement. The settlement of transactions with Visa and MasterCard cards takes place in commercial bank money (also known as demand deposits) at Bank of America and Bank of India, respectively. Many banks also issue prepaid cards with magnetic stripes that target specific customer needs, for example, payroll, foreign travel cards, gift cards, and so on.

For a large part of the population, however, cash is still the most used payment instrument. Even people with debit cards primarily use it for drawing cash from ATMs. It is estimated that 95 percent of all debit card transactions by value are at ATMs.

The banking system includes 91 banks with more than 70,000 branches. About 70 percent of banks have centralized account management, and these banks offer a range of electronic payment products to their customers. Table 4.1 includes data for the various payment instruments, for the period April 2008 to March 2009.

The Role of RBI

The RBI has played a leading role in the introduction of technological innovations in retail payments, such as using MICR technology in paper-based clearing in the 1980s and piloting a check truncation project in 2008. The Payments and Settlement Systems Act (P&SSA) of 2007 empowered the RBI to directly control all payments and settlement systems operators. All payment and settlement system operators need to apply to RBI for a payment system operator license. In accordance with

Table 4.1   Instruments for Payments and Money Transfer (volume/value)

Instrument	Volume of transactions (millions)	Value (Rs billions)
Checks[a]	1,396.00	124,612
ECS Credit[a]	88.40	975
ECS Debit[a]	160.00	670
NEFT[a]	32.00	2520
RTGS Interbank	2.15	411,358
RTGS Customer initiated[b]	11.23	200,041
Credit Cards (at POS terminals)	260.00	654
Debit Cards (at POS Terminals)	128.00	185

Source: RBI 2010.
Note: ECS = Electronic Clearing Service; NEFT = National Electronic Fund Transfer; POS = point of sale; RTGS = Real-Time Gross Settlement.
a. These instrument could be used for remittances.
b. This is also used by MTOs to pay their principal agents and by the principal agents to pay their subagents.

this legislation, Visa, MasterCard, Western Union (WU), and others have taken a license for their operations in India.

To provide a common retail payment infrastructure, banks in India, with the support of the RBI, have recently established a not-for-profit company called National Payment Corporation of India (NPCIL). NPCIL is expected to initially focus on establishing a domestic payment cards network for ATMs and POS usage. It is possible that NPCIL also might leverage its infrastructure to operate the check clearing and other retail payment systems. To reduce costs and to encourage the use of electronic payment instruments, the RBI recently waived the service charges for ECS, NEFT, and RTGS transactions and requires the banks to offer these payment services at no charge to customers. The RBI has prohibited banks from charging customers for ATM usage at both the banks' own ATMs and at other banks ATMs.

New Developments

Many banks have launched rural banking projects to provide services to the rural poor. Such schemes usually use a network of business correspondents (BCs) equipped with a smart card–accepting POS terminal, which can record basic banking transactions: withdrawal, deposit, loan installment payment, and so on. The BCs enroll customers on behalf of banks in line with the policies of the bank. The enrolled customer is provided with a smart card that records the customer's biometric authentication parameter, basic account data (number and balance), and recent transactions. These cards can be used in an offline mode at the terminals of the BC where transactions are recorded. The BC is required to synchronize these transactions with the banks' processing systems and to settle the cash collected or disbursed with the bank branch within 48 hours.

The proliferation of mobile phones usage, even in the most remote areas and by people with low incomes, has encouraged banks in cooperation with mobile service providers to launch products that use mobile phones as an access channel to a bank account. Additionally, banks have been evaluating various mobile payment schemes, one of these schemes (mChek) launched by banks and Visa, allows the owner to initiate payments via their mobile phone to participating merchants. Such innovative schemes have the potential to increase the efficiency and to reduce the costs of making payments by offering services in areas with underdeveloped banking infrastructure or an unbanked population. RBI recently issued guidelines for the operation of prepaid cards and mobile banking or payment services, which are described in detail later in this chapter.

Usage of the Payment Infrastructure for Remittance Services

The existing payment infrastructure offers a range of instruments for cross-border transfer and domestic disbursement of workers' remittances. Inward remittances to India largely rely on the banking channels for disbursement of funds to recipients. MTOs use an extensive network of bank agents. Banks are active in the remittance market in India. The existence of efficient interbank payment mechanisms has played an enabling role. The bank-operated remittance schemes use the NEFT and RTGS platforms to transfer funds to a recipient who does not have a banking relationship with the bank that sourced the remittance. The existence of this platform has enabled banks to market their services even to their noncustomers, thus providing multiple options to the sender. MTOs also use this platform to move funds to their agents. MTOs are not participants in these platforms, however; they have accounts at commercial banks, and these banks offer these fund transfer services to the MTOs. MTOs also can issue checks drawn on these account and request demand drafts. These paper instruments are used to transfer funds to agents, who maintain accounts at branches that are not covered by the electronic networks. The coverage of the electronic retail payment systems, however, is limited in rural and remote areas. Other alternatives are available but not on a large scale.[1]

India Post has the world's largest postal network and a wide geographic coverage, which allows easy access to post offices by the public. On average, a post office covers an area of 21.2 square kilometers and serves 7,166 people.[2] India Post plans to expand the network by opening 3,000 post offices in rural areas (India Post 2008). So far only 10,000 offices have been provided with IT solutions and Internet connections; however, plans are under way to automate all post offices within the next three years. As mentioned, India Post uses this infrastructure to offer domestic and international money orders, postal orders, and instant money transfers through its tie-up with WU. India Post is a participant in the Universal Postal Union initiative, which plans to link all post offices of member countries and use this network to offer faster remittance services. The WU is undertaking bilateral discussions with a few countries to offer international remittance services through the post offices of the respective countries. A pilot project is in progress between India and the United Arab Emirates. Specific agreements have been signed with Nepal and Bhutan for the provision of remittances services toward those countries using less onerous Know Your Customer (KYC) procedures.

Observations and Suggested Actions

To increase the proportion of remittance inflows into bank accounts, an adequate banking infrastructure (NEFT- and RTGS-enabled branches) is needed in areas with a high density of recipients. Banks in such areas should be encouraged by the RBI to automate their services, increase ATM coverage, and join the NEFT. This would enable banks to receive and disburse remittances more efficiently and would reduce cash payouts, which require maintaining an agent network. In certain remote areas with underdeveloped telecommunication infrastructure, it might not be economical to open traditional bank branches or to deploy ATMs (see box 4.1). Therefore, the banks should actively explore using BCs to disburse international remittances in these areas.

The RBI could explore with RSPs the feasibility of creating a common infrastructure for exchange of remittance instructions in the existing payment platforms like NEFT operated by RBI. Currently, banks have created proprietary interfaces with their foreign partners for processing of remittances. This common infrastructure could be made available to banks and nonbank RSPs. It would increase competition and enable these RSPs to significantly reduce their operational expenses and thus translate into a reduction in the cost of remittances. See box 4.2 for key features and benefits of the proposed common infrastructure.

Box 4.1

The Philippines: RuralNet

The Rural Bankers Association of the Philippines launched a cooperative venture of rural banks, RuralNet, to provide interconnectivity between rural banks and other players in the remittance sector, such as the central bank, urban banks, and government agencies. Through RuralNet, rural banks are electronically linked together into a national network. RuralNet can utilize any service provider's platform, and it ensures its compatibility with the local financial institution's system. RuralNet has made it possible for migrant-sending families to access various financial services at the local level. Through their local bank's connection to the RuralNet, such families can access remittance services, as well as housing or education loans and insurance products.

Source: Orozco and Fedewa 2005.

Box 4.2

Key Features and Benefits of a Common Infrastructure for Remittance Instructions

Key aspects of common infrastructure

- The NEFT system starts offering a separate transaction category for international remittance.
- For international remittance transactions in NEFT, the sending foreign institution can directly submit transactions to the NEFT system. The settlement for this transaction, however, would be completed by the foreign institution's local banking partner.
- For risk controls, the local banking partner can specify daily limits and so on.
- The local banking partner continues to be responsible for all compliance aspects.
- The local banking partner will need to approve the file submission at the NEFT system.

Key benefits

- ✓ Each domestic bank does not need to create a separate interface with the foreign partner.
- ✓ Because it is a common infrastructure, there would be considerable savings in cost.
- ✓ It enables even smaller banks to enter the market, thereby increasing competition

Source: Authors.

RBI could evaluate opportunities to connect India's payment infrastructure with those of major remittance-sending countries. These interconnections would make the remittance process extremely efficient and (if supported by supported by arrangements on currency conversions) could reduce exchange rate costs (as in the case of the interconnection between Mexico's payment infrastructure and the U.S. Automated Clearing House [ACH] system [see box 4.3]).

The authorities should encourage the automation of India Post's branches and encourage them to use the available payment infrastructure to offer remittance payment services in remote rural areas, where banks

Box 4.3

Connecting Domestic ACHs across Borders

In recent years, the Federal Reserve Banks in the United States have undertaken a number of initiatives to offer low-cost cross-border ACH services by linking the U.S. ACH system to that of several other countries. These services currently are limited to outbound transactions from the United States. Incoming transactions are prohibited until the U.S. ACH system can screen for U.S. Anti-Money Laundering (AML) / Combating the Financing of Terrorism (CFT) requirements.

In 2001, the Federal Reserve Banks in partnership with a private sector bank in Canada began offering a cross-border ACH service to Canada. The Canadian ACH service permits depository institutions in the United States to send ACH credit and debit transactions to depository institutions in Canada.

In 2003, the Federal Reserve Banks began offering a trans-Atlantic ACH service to five countries in the Western Europe (Austria, Germany, the Netherlands, Switzerland, and the United Kingdom). The trans-Atlantic ACH service is limited to credit transactions only, with transactions originated in U.S. dollars in the United States and received in the domestic currency of the European country.

In 2004, the Federal Reserve Banks and the Bank of Mexico began offering a cross-border ACH service from the United States to Mexico under the name *Directo a Mexico*. It uses the exchange rate published daily by the Bank of Mexico ("the fix"). The Federal Reserve Banks charge depository institutions in the United States less than $1.00 per payment. The Bank of Mexico does not charge banks in Mexico for the service but receives part of the fee charged by the Federal Reserve Banks. Although the vast majority of the payments are U.S. government payments to individuals in Mexico, the channel is available for use by depository institutions offering cross-border remittance services to Mexico.

Source: BIS 2007.

or nonbank remittance providers are not present. Limited automation and lack of connectivity prevents most postal offices from being used to process electronic remittances. The authorities should consider mechanisms through which India Post can participate in the electronic payment infrastructure (NEFT, ECS, and RTGS). This would enable recipients who have accounts with India Post to receive remittances directly into these accounts.

Legal and Regulatory Environment: Remittance Services Should Be Supported by a Sound, Predictable, Nondiscriminatory, and Proportionate Legal and Regulatory Framework in Relevant Jurisdictions (GP 3)

The legal and regulatory framework includes both the general legal infrastructure (such as laws relating to contracts, payments, securities, banking, debtor/creditor relationships, and insolvency) and any specific statutes, case law, regulations, or contracts (for example, payment system rules) relevant to remittances.

A *sound* framework that is well understood helps minimize the risks faced by both RSPs and their customers. A *predictable* framework is one in which it is clear which laws and regulations are relevant; which do not change with excessive frequency; and which are enforced by the authorities, including the courts, in a consistent manner. *Nondiscriminatory* refers to the legal and regulatory framework being equally applicable to different types of RSPs insofar as they are providing equivalent services. This promotes a level playing field and encourages competition. Because remittance services are provided by many different types of service providers, a functional rather than institutional framework may be desirable to reduce different treatment of service providers offering similar services. Given that, in many countries, bank and nonbank RSPs may be governed by different, well-established legal and regulatory frameworks, it is important to ensure that equivalent rights and obligations (with respect to remittance services) exist regardless of which body of law applies to these institutions.

A remittance involves at least two jurisdictions: the sending and the receiving countries. The authorities of a given country have a direct influence only on the framework in their own country. Therefore, cooperation with the authorities of other countries becomes necessary.

Payments-Related Legislation and Regulations

India's legal framework for payment systems and instruments has been evolving to meet the needs of the market. Several important payments-related acts and amendments have been adopted recently, which have created a sound legal framework (in line with international standards) and have contributed to the safe functioning and provision of payment systems and services in India. The key elements required for interbank payment systems (such as settlement finality, legal recognition of netting, and protection of collateral) are already in place, and the regulations and guidelines are predictable and well publicized.

Several acts and bylaws (RBI regulations, circulars, and guidelines) that regulate various aspects of the financial system are relevant to payments and specifically to international remittances. Under the provisions of the Reserve Bank of India Act, 1934, the RBI, as the central bank of the country, is empowered to make statutory regulations with respect to fund transfers through electronic means between banks or between banks and other financial institutions. The newly adopted P&SSA establishes a sound legal framework for functioning of payment systems in the country. The act addresses a number of issues, such as the following:

- Designating the RBI as the authority to regulate payment and settlement systems
- Making an authorization by RBI compulsory to operate payment systems
- Empowering RBI to regulate and supervise payment systems, by issuing regulations and directives, determining standards, and requiring regular reporting of authorized payment system operators
- Empowering RBI to conduct inspections of payment systems operators
- Providing for settlement to be final and irrevocable from the moment at which the payment obligations (funds, securities or foreign exchange) of the participants are determined
- Recognizing bilateral or multilateral netting

The Payment and Settlement Systems Regulation, 2008, which was issued under article 38 of the P&SSA, describes the authorization procedure, requirements for granting authorization, and the reporting requirements for payment system operators. Other relevant regulations include the following: the Negotiable Instruments Act, 1881, governing noncash paper-based payment systems, which was amended to provide for electronic checks imaging and check truncation; the Information Technology Act, 2000; and the Indian Contract Act, 1872. The legislation varies according to the nature of the RSP (bank versus nonbank). Banks are regulated by the RBI under the Banking Regulation Act, 1949. Nonbank entities offering remittance services entities are regulated under the Foreign Exchange Management Act (FEMA).

The Circular on Mobile Banking Transactions in India—Operating Guidelines for Banks, 2008, issued under article 18 of the P&SSA—allows banks that are licensed and supervised in India and that have implemented core banking solutions to offer mobile banking services.

The guidelines allow banks to provide such services only domestically in rupees. The report of the recent Inter-Ministerial Group on the Delivery of Basic Financial Services Using Mobile Phones (GoI 2010) provides a framework for the use of mobile phones to offer banking services, including money transfer services. The RBI established requirements for these services to meet minimum technology and security standards. The main features of these guidelines are as follows:

- Allow only banks to offer mobile banking/payment solutions
- Specify customer registration requirements
- Establish guidelines for technology standards
- Specify customer grievance handling mechanisms
- Specify KYC norms

In 2009, the RBI issued guidelines for paper and prepaid payment instruments, such as prepaid cards, Internet wallets, e-purse, mobile accounts, paper vouchers, and so on. The guidelines allow banks and licensed nonbank financial companies to issue open-loop prepaid instruments, whereas other entities can offer only proprietary closed-loop prepaid instruments. The main features of these guidelines are as follows:

- Enable nonbanks to issue only proprietary closed-loop prepaid cards
- Specify eligibility criteria, capital requirement, AML compliance, KYC requirements, safekeeping of customer funds, and customer grievances handling
- Limit Indian rupee–denominated prepaid instruments to a maximum value of Rs 50,000
- Relax KYC norms for lower denomination closed-loop cards
- Enable banks to appoint BCs to source and service prepaid cards

To increase the outreach of the banking sector, the RBI established (in a circular dated January 2006) the rules and criteria for banks to appoint agents (BCs). The activities permitted for BCs include disbursing low-value remittances. BCs can be nongovernmental organizations (NGOs), microfinance institutions (MFIs), co-operative societies, and designated individuals. Banks are responsible to ensure that all regulations and requirements are met by their agents and are required to regularly submit statistical information (on inflows and outflows, among others), as well as information about new agent additions to RBI. In November 2009, the RBI widened the list of individuals and organizations eligible for appointment as

BCs to include petrol pump owners, retired teachers, and *kirana*[3] shops, insurance agents, agents of government-run small savings schemes, and self-help groups linked to banks.

Foreign-Exchange and Remittances-Related Legislation and Regulations

FEMA is the most relevant legislation to international remittances, and was enacted to promote the development and maintenance of a foreign exchange (FX) market in India. As discussed in chapter 3, FEMA empowers the RBI to regulate, among other things, foreign currency payments into and out of India. FEMA regulates only entities established in India for the purposes of conducting foreign exchange operations, including cross-border remittance operations to and from the country. Only Authorized Dealers (ADs) can perform the foreign exchange operations and services stipulated in the act, and they require licensing from RBI to do so (see chapter 3 for eligibility criteria).

The FX Department at RBI has created two specific approval regimes for provision for remittance services: the Rupee Drawing Arrangement (RDA) and the Money Transfer Service Scheme (MTSS). Banks are allowed to offer remittance services in partnership with banks in other countries without express permission from RBI. Banks do need to take the approval of the FX Department of RBI, under the RDA scheme for tie-ups with nonbanking institutions in the sending countries. Apart from banks, AD IIs and Full-Fledged Money Changers (FFMCs) are allowed to offer remittance services. These nonbanking entities need to offer remittance services in accordance with the MTSS and need express approval from the FX Department of RBI. The key features of the two regimes are presented in chapter 3.

As of July 2009, 40 Indian banks working in collaboration with 70 exchange houses in sending countries were authorized to operate under the RDA scheme, and 11 overseas principals in collaboration with 26 Indian principal agents were permitted to offer remittance services under the MTSS. The number of subagents exceeds 100,000, including branches of commercial banks. The RBI is considering amending the eligibility criteria for agents. This proposal is under discussion with the government. The amendments will include due-diligence measures, requirements for regular external audits, and higher capital requirements.

The MTSS restricts the number of inward cash-to-cash or account-to-cash payments that can be received by a single individual to 12 payments a year of not more than US$2,500 per payment. Another limitation is that the maximum payout that can be paid in cash is limited to Rs 50,000. Any amount exceeding this limit has to be paid by check, draft, or payment order, or credited directly to the beneficiary's account.

As for the tax regime, foreign exchange conversion is subject to a service tax. This service tax is applicable on the foreign exchange conversion fee, and not on the remittance amount (however, the conversion fee needs to be a reasonable fee and cannot be zero). This service tax is not applicable to interbank foreign exchange transactions, but it is applicable to all other transactions. Therefore, in remittance schemes operated by banks (including RDA schemes), foreign exchange flows into India appear as bank-to-bank foreign exchange transfers, and hence the service tax is not applied to these transactions. On the other hand, the transfer of funds from the Money Transfer Operator (MTO) to its nonbank principal agents (under the MTSS) is treated as a foreign exchange transaction of a banking customer, and hence the service tax applies.

Finally, the RBI specifically prohibits nonbanks from offering domestic remittance services, and restricts the offering of these services to banks and post offices. As a consequence, many institutions (such as MFIs) and mobile phone operators are prohibited from the provision of remittance services.

Observations and Suggested Actions

The RBI could consider reviewing the limits on the frequency of remittance inflows through the MTSS to ensure that they meet the needs of the users. The limit might be prohibitive, for example, in the case that the beneficiary receives remittances from more than one family member working abroad. Given that an industrywide record of the remittances received does not exist, it is impossible to enforce this requirement. A sender can use another MTO to send remittances in case the recipient exceeds the yearly limit. This requirement might force the sender to use another MTO than their preferred (and cheaper) MTO.

The RBI could consider reviewing the impact of the service tax on foreign exchange conversion for remittance services. The differing applicability of this tax for bank-operated remittance services and MTO-operated services, while not affecting the cost structure of the MTOs significantly, does not create a level playing field.

The RBI could evaluate opportunities for leveraging the agent networks of MTOs for domestic remittances. Significant domestic migration occurs within India, which has created a demand for domestic remittance services. The domestic remittance market is serviced only by banks and post offices. The money transfer services of post office are used quite extensively, but they remain unpopular for time-critical transfers. The unbanked internal migrants rely on community arrangements, often involving physical transportation of cash. The opportunities to improve the remittance services available for domestic migrants could include the following: (a) allowing MTOs to leverage the existing agent network for offering domestic remittance services, and (b) allowing banks to tie up with MTOs to create domestic remittance products along the lines of the RDA scheme. Such mechanisms could greatly improve domestic migrants' families' timely and reliable access to funds, and could enable the MTOs to spread the agent network costs over more transactions, thus resulting in overall lower costs for all remittances.

Market Structure and Competition: Competitive Market Conditions, Including Appropriate Access to Domestic Payments Infrastructures, Should Be Fostered in the Remittance Industry (GP 4)

The efficiency of remittance services depends on the existence of a competitive business environment. Competitive markets can limit monopolistic practices and lead to lower prices and improved service levels. One significant barrier to entry is the availability of potential agents as some RSPs bind their agents to exclusive contracts, thereby blocking new entrants.

To provide remittance services, RSPs usually need to be able to use the domestic payment infrastructure. Access to this infrastructure can be direct or indirect (by using the payment services provided by institutions having direct access). Both forms of access are capable of providing RSPs with suitable payment services. Whichever form access takes, it is important that it is available to RSPs on a fair and competitive basis, because access to the payment infrastructure may be a factor in their ability to compete.

Market Structure
The market for remittances in India is dominated by banks, with around an 80 percent share of recorded remittances inflows. The remittance services offered by the banks are *exclusively* geared toward remittances into bank accounts, either with the same bank or at some other bank. The remittance services offered by MTOs are geared toward cash payout to the recipient. Remittances initiated using bank-operated schemes, tend to

be larger (in fact, they are estimated to be almost twice as large) and less frequent than those initiated through MTOs.

The profile of the senders using bank-operated schemes tends to be skewed toward white-collar workers, whereas the typical sender using an MTO-operated scheme is a blue-collar worker. The profile of the recipients also has a bearing on which scheme is used. Recipients receiving remittances from MTO-operated schemes appear to be predominantly unbanked. Banks, in general, appear to be reluctant to offer cash-to-cash remittance services largely because of AML/CFT concerns. Banks do not consider this market segment as attractive and do not value low-income migrants and the receiving households as customers. This may be changing, however, as banks start to appreciate the potential of cross-selling other financial services to senders and receivers of even low-value transfers. Banks using the RDA scheme have made significant inroads in attracting senders that are unable to access the banking channels in the sending country and are more comfortable in using exchange houses. Even in this case, however, banks offer only credit-to-account remittances. So from a sender's perspective if the recipient needs cash, the sender would necessarily have to use the MTO scheme.

Given these distinct customer segments and the reluctance of banks to offer cash-to-cash services, the bank-operated and MTO-operated schemes generally are seen as being two different products, and not as competing against each other. The reasons for this segmentation could be based on (a) the preference of the recipients, which is likely determined by their level of access to the banking system; (b) the level of financial literacy of the sender and recipient; and (c) the time-criticality of the remittance.[4]

Competition in the Market for the Provision of Remittance Services

The level of competition is very high in the bank-operated schemes, with many banks active in the market. The leaders in this segment include ICICI Bank, SBI, Federal Bank, HDFC Bank, Bank of India, Citibank, and Bank of Baroda. The level of competition in the MTO segment is limited, with WU dominating this segment with close to 80 percent of the MTO market. MoneyGram and the UAE Exchange are the other active players in the MTO segment. This differing level of competition could be one of the reasons for the difference in the average cost of remittance using these two schemes.

Some international MTOs require their agents to contractually agree on exclusivity, whereby the agent is prohibited from becoming an agent for another MTO. This practice has allowed MTOs to bind organizations with large branch networks to provide only their remittance services. This creates a significant barrier for other MTOs to expand their agent network and, consequently, affects their ability to compete effectively. This practice could enable such MTOs to charge higher prices for their remittance services.

The Competition Commission of India (CCI) regulates and monitors the adherence to the Competition Act. The Competition Act was enacted in 2003 and subsequently was amended in 2007. This act contains provisions to prohibit anticompetitive agreements and abuse of dominant positions, and includes the power to regulate mergers and acquisitions that could curtail competition. The CCI became fully operational in May 2009.

Access to the Payment Infrastructure

MTOs are able to access the payments infrastructure in India, as customers of banks. This level of access is sufficient for the conduct of their remittance business. Given the large number of banks, MTOs have several choices, which has enabled MTOs to get a high level of service and competitive pricing for these payment services. India Post currently is not a direct participant in the NEFT and RTGS systems, but it can access these systems as a corporate customer of a bank.

Observations and Suggested Actions

The RBI and the CCI could study the impact of exclusivity agreements and consider banning these agreements. Exclusive agreements impede the ability of excluded MTOs to expand their agent network and could enable the exclusive MTO (which has secured a large agent network) to charge higher prices for remittances.

The RBI could consider creating an enabling framework for banks to offer cash-to-cash remittance services (similar to those provided by MTOs) by establishing an appropriate level of requirements for them to create competitive offerings in this segment of the market as well.

Governance and Risk Management: Remittance Services Should Be Supported by Appropriate Governance and Risk Management Practices (GP 5)

Appropriate governance and risk management practices by RSPs can improve the safety and soundness of remittance services and help protect consumers. Governance structures can help RSPs meet their fiduciary obligations to their customers. RSPs should strive to adopt governance standards according to both their countries' legal requirements and best practices.

The international remittance industry faces legal, financial, operational, fraud, and reputational risks. In establishing risk control measures to protect themselves from these risks, RSPs should conduct risk-level assessments to ensure that proposed risk control measures are appropriate to the level of the risks and the size of the business. In doing so, they should take appropriate steps to protect themselves and their customers against risks arising from their operations in different jurisdictions, in particular, those with shortcomings in their legal and regulatory framework.

Governance in India's Remittance Market

The FX Department of the RBI is responsible for the oversight of the overall remittances market. Commercial banks, co-operative banks, and nonbanks are supervised by different departments of the RBI. Commercial banks are supervised by the Department of Banking Operation; co-operative banks are supervised by the National Bank for Agriculture and Rural Development (NABARD), a subsidiary of RBI; nonbanks (AD II and FFMC) are supervised by the FX Department; and the MTOs operating MTSSs are supervised by the Payment Systems Department of the RBI. These supervisory departments are tasked with ensuring adherence to the guidelines set by the FX Department to conduct remittance business under the RDA schemes and MTSSs. RSPs are required to regularly submit statistical information and to report any new subagent agreement to RBI. RBI regulates only the agents. The RSP is responsible for subagents' adherence to RBI rules and guidelines. Subagents can be grocery stores, gas stations, and others.

The Prevention of Money Laundering Act of 2002 (PMLA) requires all banks to adhere to CFT and AML requirements. This act has been amended to require all MTOs to adhere to the same requirements. Proportionally relaxed KYC requirements are in place for cash-to-cash transactions under Rs 50,000.

Risk Management in India's Remittance Market

Liquidity and credit risks seem to be adequately addressed in the Indian market. Under the RDA scheme, the foreign partner is required to prefund the rupee Vostro account with the Indian bank before disbursement to the recipient. Under the MTSS, principal agents are required to collect collateral from the MTO, equivalent to three days' worth of transactions or US\$50,000 whichever is higher. In addition to the collateral requirement, at the time of approval, principal agents are required to maintain a minimum capital requirement based on their projected business volume. Specific guidelines or monitoring requirements of the agent networks do not exist. This results in some agents of RSPs assuming credit and liquidity risks as they disburse funds to the beneficiary before they receive the necessary funds from the RSP. This is particularly the case in the cash-to-cash segment of the market. Currently, these exposures are not deemed to be systemic, and RSPs seem to have backup procedures in place to provide extra cash liquidity to their agents and subagents. Nonetheless, the possible reputational risk must not be underestimated.

Specific guidelines related to fraud and operational risk management for remittance services do not exist. For banks providing remittance services, these risks are covered as part of the detailed RBI guidelines on governance and risk management that govern their overall banking operations. MTOs, on the other hand, are not subject to such requirements although many have established a range of practices, including disaster recovery planning, policies of agent sign-up, due diligence of agents, transaction monitoring, periodic training, and agent network audits.

Observations and Suggested Actions

The RBI could consider developing a guideline on governance and risk management requirements to be followed by nonbank MTSS principal agents and the MTOs. As mentioned, nonbank MTSS principal agents have designed certain in-house mechanisms. However, to ensure certain minimum standards for governance and risk management, the RBI should consider developing relevant guidelines for the nonbank MTSS principal agents, which would (a) require MTSS principal agents to have a risk management policy for operational, liquidity, and credit risks; (b) require MTSS principal agents to establish policies for enrolling, training, and monitoring their subagents; and (c) require MTSS principal agents to audit their agents and subagents periodically and make them responsible for compliance with all prevalent rules.

The Role of Remittance Service Providers: To Participate Actively in the Implementation of the GPs

RSPs should strive to offer competitive services that meet their customers' needs. While competing on services, however, RSPs should cooperate on core infrastructure to take advantage of economies of scale and network effects and thus reduce processing costs. As payment service providers, they have a particular responsibility to ensure that both they and any capturing or disbursing agents with whom they contract are adhering to applicable laws and regulations. They should implement appropriate governance and risk management processes to improve the safety and soundness of their services and to meet their fiduciary responsibilities to their customers.

Status in India

There is some degree of cooperation among banks in India through the Indian Banks Association (IBA). The degree of cooperation, however, has not yet been extended to the area of performance standards and minimum service levels for bank customers. For the nonbank remittances business, the MTSS principal agents in India do not have any association. Given that all principal agents also are FFMCs or banks, the Foreign Exchange Dealers Association of India (FEDAI) and IBA occasionally are used to discuss issues relating to money transfer services.

Banks and MTSS agents in India are legally obligated to comply with official standards in the area of AML/CFT and to report the details of suspect transactions and activities to the RBI's Financial Intelligence Unit (FIU). Many banks and nonbank MTSS principal agents have well-established AML/CFT monitoring mechanism, with a designated officer responsible for this function with a direct reporting line to the organization's chief executive.

Observations and Suggested Actions

All RSPs should consider developing industry-wide common minimum standards and encourage all agents to have appropriate governance structures in place. Some important aspects that should be covered include the following: (a) transaction timelines; (b) details to be included in receipts; (c) disclosure of exchange rates and fees; (d) complaint procedures and resolution schemes, including the consequences of exceeding transfer times; (e) safety measures, including due provisions for safeguarding customer funds that are in the pipeline; and (f) risk management measures. IBA and FEDAI should consider forming a joint committee to discuss remittance-related issues and raise awareness about the GPs.

RSPs should undertake efforts to weed out agents perpetrating fraud. This can be addressed by setting up a blacklisting mechanism whereby agents information is shared within the association and fraudulent agents are debarred from working with other members.

RSPs have a role to play in engaging in ground-level education of remittance recipients to promote the use of efficient payment instruments and the use of broader financial services. RSPs can make concerted efforts to increase the awareness of the senders and recipients about remittance-sending options, as well as the various options available for receiving remittances and the potential financial products linked to the remittance inflows (see the section on leveraging remittances to improve financial access).

The Role of Public Authorities: To Evaluate What Action to Take to Achieve the Public Policy Objectives through Implementation of the GPs

The relevant authorities need to have appropriate powers and resources to implement the public policy objectives stated in the GPs. The authorities have various tools at their disposal, including the following: monitoring, dialogue with the private sector, and the provision of information to the public. In cases in which implementation of these objectives involves multiple domestic authorities, public policy makers should ensure that domestic policies are coordinated and that the authorities cooperate on a policy and implementation. Cooperation at an international level— whether bilateral cooperation between central banks of sending and receiving countries, regional cooperation, or global cooperation—also is useful.

Public Authorities in India's Remittance Marketplace

In India, different aspects of remittance-related activities fall under the jurisdiction of various authorities, such as the RBI, the Ministry of Finance (MoF), the MOIA, and, to a limited extent, the CCI and the Ministry of Consumer Affairs. The MoF, the MOIA, and the RBI are at the center of the efforts to improve remittance services and individually and collectively have strived to improve market conditions for remittances.

The RBI's departments have cooperated effectively to support an orderly and efficient market for remittances. As regulator of the market and payment system overseer, RBI has ensured that legislation is evolving continually to keep pace with the developments of the market. The payment system infrastructure has been improved to meet the needs of economy. Innovative methodologies have been created to estimate the number of migrants and volumes of remittance flows. Data collection is reliable and provides the relevant information on crucial aspects of the market.

The MOIA was established in 2004 to "promote, nurture and sustain a mutually beneficial and symbiotic relationship between India and overseas Indians" (MOIA 2009). It has four functional service divisions: Diaspora Services, Financial Services, Emigration Services, and Management Services, and it is charged with all matters relating to Overseas Indians. MOIA's focus is to create an institutional framework to support networks with and among Overseas Indians. Such institutional framework currently consists of the following government and nonprofit entities: (a) Overseas Indian Facilitation Center, which serves as a one-stop shop for economic engagement, investment, and business; (b) India Development Foundation, which facilitates the Diasporas' philanthropic investment into India's development efforts; (c) the Indian Council of Overseas Employment, which provides strategic analysis on matters related to overseas employment markets; (d) Global Indian Network of Knowledge, an electronic platform to leverage the expertise and skills of overseas Indians; (e) the prime minister's Global Advisory Council, to draw on the best overseas Indian minds; and (f) the Overseas Indian Center at the Indian Missions in Washington, DC, and Abu Dhabi, the United Arab Emirates, which serve as field formations on matters relating to overseas Indians.

The MOIA is responsible for promoting trade and investments, emigration, education, financial literacy, culture, health, and all the issues related to Overseas Indians. Policy interventions and bilateral cooperation with destination countries have led to the creation of several activities and agreements aimed at supporting and assisting the Overseas Indians. Among them are the agreements with the Gulf Cooperation Council (GCC) countries and Malaysia for the benefit of skilled and semiskilled workers and the negotiations with several countries worldwide for assisting Indian professionals. Specific labor mobility partnerships have been discussed with European Union (EU) countries to enhance employment exchange. Other specific programs include awareness campaigns on the risks of illegal migration, predeparture orientation and skill training for migrant workers, legal assistance abroad, counseling and training, and creation of manuals for predeparture orientation in understandable and multilingual versions.[5]

The MOIA has put in place a comprehensive set of policies and mechanisms to provide support and assistance to the migrants. Several of these measures are beneficial to the improvement of the market for remittances, such as the establishment of the Office of Protector General of Migrants, predeparture training booklets, helplines, consular offices, and increased cooperation with foreign counterparts in the analysis of migration processes and in the establishment of periodic exchanges of information and dialogue.

Observations and Suggested Action

The RBI and MOIA could collaborate in the production and publication of tables with comparative information on costs and other relevant variables, relating to remittance services. This information would be of great help to the migrants and recipients. For this information to be as effective as possible, all relevant information channels should be used, including printed leaflets, newspapers, Internet, contact centers, and so on. Information should be made available in India and in the main sending countries through consular offices, migrant organizations, associations, and others.[6]

RBI could collect more detailed information related to remittances (from banks, MTSS principal agents, and MTO agents) and increase the analysis and synthesis of the data collected. Currently, RBI only collects the list of new subagents and the transaction volume data from the MTSS operators. Additional information related to transaction patterns could be collected, such as the number of recipients, the number of transactions, regional distribution of the recipients, the top few subagents and their transaction volumes, and source countries. This would enhance the data available for analysis and assist RBI in its supervisory and oversight activities.

The MOIA should consider including more information related to remittance services, such as payment options and consumer protection measures in the communication materials that MOIA currently prepares for briefing migrants. In the same vein, MOIA could consider stepping up its migration- and remittance-related data collection. The data could be collected when providing services to migrants and their families. The data collected could include awareness of the remittance options, use of remittances, skill level, reasons for migration, and so on.

Finally, to further leverage India's large Diaspora, the Indian authorities can resume their issuance of Diaspora bonds to finance long-term investments in infrastructure or projects with high social value in India.

Policy Recommendations to Improve Financial Access through Remittance-Linked Financial Products

Remittances have the potential to alleviate poverty when they are channeled into savings, home improvements, building assets, and business growth. The demand- and supply-side evidence indicates that remittance-linked financial products in India are not yet readily available or well targeted for financial inclusion. Financial institutions seem to be keen on learning more about this market and developing appropriate products. The following recommendations aim to leverage the use of remittances to improve financial access.

Improving migrants' access to bank accounts. Banking access of migrants and recipients can be improved by (a) issuing identification cards (such as the Mexican *Matrícula Consular*) that are accepted by banks for opening accounts, and by (b) encouraging source country banks to open branches in destination countries. These institutions, in turn, can benefit as the availability of remittance services may attract customers for their savings and loan products. Incentives such as higher interest rate on remittance-linked savings accounts or offering an extra premium for accounts that maintain some minimum balance can further attract recipients to the banks (see appendix C for the Mexican experience in banking migrants).

Developing appropriate products. One of the most effective ways to expand financial access through remittance-linked financial products is through the development of appropriate financial products that can bring low-income recipients, especially unbanked ones, into the financial system (see box 4.4 for Guatemala's experience). Although regular financial products might be used by the remittance recipients, their lack of awareness about financial products, self-exclusion from the formal financial institution, and tedious application procedures often deter potential customers from approaching financial institutions. The challenge for financial institutions thus lies in leveraging the remittance link of the recipients as their entry point to access other financial products. Linking the recipients' savings accounts to a credit line can help expand access to loan services. Examples of the remittance-linked loan product include *Banco salvadoreno*'s (El Salvador) loan product, which allows remittance recipients to receive loans up to 80 percent of the remittance amount received in the previous six months.

Indian authorities could offer incentives to financial institutions to expand financial access through remittance-linked financial products. For example, remittance-linked loan products for unbanked customers could be considered as priority-sector lending, lower provisioning requirements could be offered for such loans, or a demonstration institution could lead the development and promotion of remittance-linked financial products. Assessment studies that identify the needs of the potential customers, as well as workshops and seminars on international best practices in introducing remittance-linked financial products, should be undertaken.

Box 4.4

Savings-Led Approach to Increase Financial Services for Remittance Recipients

The World Council of Credit Unions and the Guatemalan National Credit Union Federation, with support from U.S. Agency for International Development, ran a pilot program in Guatemala from 2006 to 2008. The purpose of this pilot was to increase remittance recipients' access to formal savings accounts and other financial services. The pilot program worked on three fronts: product development, marketing and branding, and back-end systems development.

Product development: A special savings product was designed for remittance recipients. The goal was to enable recipients to save a portion of their remittances by allowing them to deposit them directly into interest-bearing accounts. More than 2,822 remittance recipients signed up for it even before the product was publicized, 1,060 remittance recipients became credit union members, and 10 percent of new members opened deposit account.

Marketing and branding: Through a nationwide promotion campaign, the benefits of credit union membership and availability of various financial products were popularized among the recipients. Senders of remittances were encouraged to use credit unions to send remittances.

Back-end systems development: An information technology platform was created to capture information about recipients and senders that is useful in marketing and cross-selling financial products. The new system tracks the occupation of the recipient, relationship to the sender, amount of time the sender has resided in the United States, and the frequency and amount of remittances received. This information is useful for credit unions when evaluating loans for recipients who do not have a steady source of income apart from remittances.

As a result of the program, credit union membership and remittance flows into credit union accounts increased. Of the total 65,535 credit union remittance recipients in Guatemala, more than 3,350 recipients opened remittance-linked direct deposit accounts, and 1,378 new recipients have joined the credit unions, of whom 12.5 percent opened the direct deposit accounts.

Source: USAID 2009.

In addition, the authorities could consider allowing MFIs to enter the remittance market and to distribute remittances especially in rural areas, once they get the proper licensing and enforce the required norms and regulations. Finally, India Post should be encouraged to leverage its large branch network and financial product offering to provide efficient remittance services and remittance-linked financial products. India Post could do this by automating its branches, establishing links to India's other retail payment networks, and leveraging new payment mechanisms like prepaid cards.

Use of technology. Many countries have introduced technology in providing remittance and other financial services. The G-cash product in the Philippines and M-pesa in Kenya are two of the most successful examples of providing remittance and other financial services through mobile phones. In addition, governments in many countries have designed policy measures to facilitate the use of technology in financial inclusion through remittances. The State Bank of Pakistan, for example, recently issued guidelines for three models of branchless banking: (a) banks can work with telecom providers to offer financial services to the current customer base of that provider, (b) banks can offer mobile phone banking services to their own customers using mobile connection of any telecom, and (c) a group of banks can provide financial services in cooperation with telecoms. With more than 600 million mobile phone subscribers in India, Indian policy makers can exploit the wide usage of mobile phones to expand financial access by promoting new partnerships and linkages between financial institutions and mobile phone operators (GoI 2010; World Bank 2009).

Notes

1. Domestic remittances within India are estimated to be large and remain an under-researched area.
2. This compares favorably with the United States, where a post office covers an area of 259.25 square kilometers and serves 8,029 people, and China, where a post office covers an area of 145.59 square kilometers and serves 19,962 people.
3. *Kirana* shops are small stand-alone shops.
4. Low-income workers are more likely to use the services of MTOs for a variety of reasons, including the following: MTOs have (a) more convenient opening hours and days, which allow the migrants to reach collection points after normal working hours; (b) insufficient coverage of collecting and disbursing banking infrastructure in the sending country; (c) inhibitions about approaching a bank; (d) limited financial literacy and inability to comply with the minimum requirements to open an account; and (e) lengthy KYC procedures.

5. For further information on the activities of the MOIA, see http://www.moia
   .gov.in.
6. This can be done based on the methodology developed by the World Bank to
   track remittance costs of leading providers in a number of sending-receiving
   country pairs, which is maintained at http://remittanceprices.worldbank.org.

References

BIS (Bank for International Settlements). 2007. "General Principles for
International Remittance Services." Committee on Payment and Settlement
Systems Publication 76, BIS Basel, Switzerland.

GoI (Government of India). 2010. "Framework for Delivery of Basic Financial
Services Using Mobile Phone," Report of the Inter-ministerial Group, Delhi.

India Post. 2008. "Annual Report 2007–2008." Available on http://www.indiapost
.gov.in_(accessed on October 1, 2009).

MOIA (Ministry of Overseas Indian Affairs). 2009. *Annual Report 2008–2009.*
Available at http://moia.gov.in (accessed October 1, 2009).

Orozco, M., and R. Fedewa. 2005. "Regional Integration: Trends and Patterns of
Remittance Flows within South East Asia." Report prepared for the South
East Asia Workers Remittance Study, Washington DC.

RBI (Reserve Bank of India). 2010. "NRI Deposits: Outstanding/Inflows and
Outflows." *Reserve Bank of India Bulletin,* March 10.

USAID (United States Agency for International Development). 2009. "Integrating
Remittance Recipients into the Financial System." Field Brief USAID 5,
Washington, DC.

World Bank. 2009. *Bringing Finance to Pakistan's Poor: A Study on Access to Finance
for the Underserved and Small Enterprises.* Directions in Development Series,
Washington, DC: World Bank.

The Other Side of the Story: Migration to India and Outward Remittances from India

To provide an overall picture of India's remittances, it is important to look at migration to Indian and outward remittance flows from, India Data on migration to India vary and are inaccurate because of the large number of irregular migrants. According to the Ministry of Overseas Indian Affairs (MOIA), India is home to an estimated 20 million immigrants; many of them are irregular migrants. The World Bank estimates for 2005 ranked India eighth among the top 10 immigration countries in the world with 5.7 million migrants (around 0.5 percent of the population) (see figure A1.1).

India is an important destination country for migrants from the neighboring countries of Bangladesh, Nepal, Pakistan, and Sri Lanka (World Bank 2008 presents data for 2005). Migration from Bangladesh, Nepal, and Sri Lanka to India is mainly dominated by unskilled and semiskilled workers. In addition to limited border management, economic factors such as employment opportunities and demand for cheap labor, as well as cultural affinities and migration histories of families and villages, have driven migration from these countries to India. Most of the migration from Pakistan to India happened during the time of partition.

Figure A1.1   Top 10 Immigration Countries, 2005

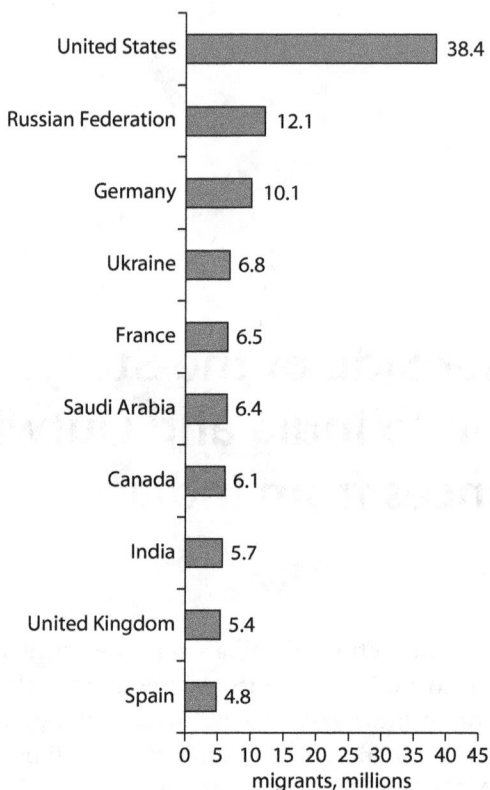

Bar chart showing migrants (millions):
- United States: 38.4
- Russian Federation: 12.1
- Germany: 10.1
- Ukraine: 6.8
- France: 6.5
- Saudi Arabia: 6.4
- Canada: 6.1
- India: 5.7
- United Kingdom: 5.4
- Spain: 4.8

x-axis: migrants, millions (0 to 45)

Source: World Bank 2008.

Migrants from Bangladesh account for the largest number. The estimates of irregular migration from Bangladesh to India range from 5 million to 20 million (Kumar 2008). These migrants are concentrated in the state of West Bengal and the North Eastern States, notably Assam. In addition, megacities like Delhi and Mumbai also attract Bangladeshi migrants in search of better economic opportunities. Most of these migrants work as unskilled or semiskilled laborers and domestic servants.

The India-Nepal border is wide open to people movement, making Nepalese the second-largest migrant community in India. Estimates about the number of Nepalese migrants in India vary from 1 million to 3 million. Close to 90 percent of Nepalese migrants are concentrated in five Indian states: Assam, Bihar, Uttarakhand, Uttar Pradesh, and West

Bengal. Most Nepalese migrants are unskilled seasonal workers in agriculture or construction. Some Nepalese also serve in the Indian army.

As for remittance outflows, figure A1.2 presents the top 10 remittance-sending countries in 2008. Not surprisingly, the United States tops the list with outward remittances reaching more than US$47 billion in 2008; the Russian Federation is a distant second with US$26.1 billion. Saudi Arabia and Malaysia are the two nonmember countries of the Organisation for Economic Co-operation and Development (OECD) among the top 10 sending countries. India does not make the top 10 (it ranked 31st in 2008 with US$1.58 billion in outward remittances).

India's share in outward remittances has been increasing over time. With more than US$1.58 billion in official outward remittances in 2008, India is fast becoming a large remittance-sending country (see

Figure A1.2   Top 10 Remittance-Sending Countries, 2008

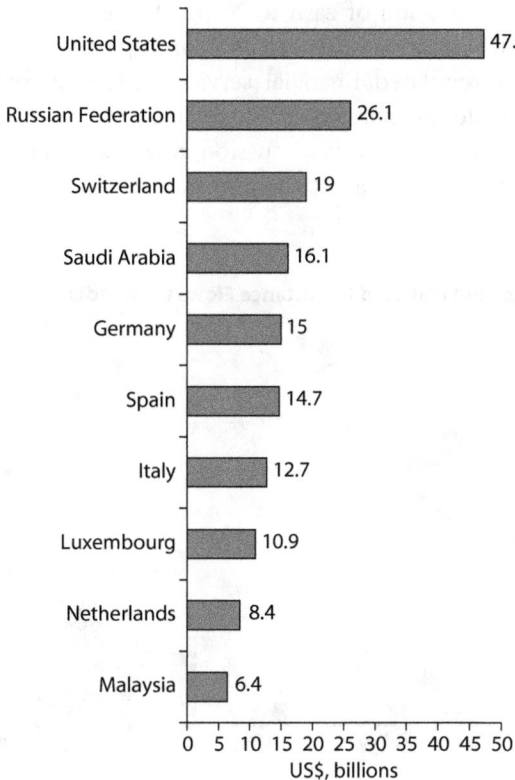

Country	US$, billions
United States	47.2
Russian Federation	26.1
Switzerland	19
Saudi Arabia	16.1
Germany	15
Spain	14.7
Italy	12.7
Luxembourg	10.9
Netherlands	8.4
Malaysia	6.4

Source: World Bank 2009.

figure A1.3).[1] The true size of outbound remittance flows is believed
to be much larger, however, because of unrecorded flows from irregular
and undocumented migrants to India.

To enable low-cost and fast remittances from India to Nepal, in January
2008, the Reserve Bank of India (RBI) authorized two Indian banks, State
Bank of India (SBI) and Punjab National Bank (PNB), to act as gateways
for remittances from India to Nepal. All the banks originating Nepal-
bound remittances are required to route the transactions to SBI and PNB
using a designated transaction type in National Electronic Fund Transfer
(NEFT). These banks then transfer the funds and forward the information
to their affiliate banks SBI Nepal and Everest Bank, respectively. These
two local Nepalese banks, in turn, have partnered with a Nepalese Money
Transfer Operator (MTO) for onward cash disbursement to the recipients.
This scheme is hardly used, however, because of the unattractive revenue
model and lack of interest from the banks. Therefore, remittances through
this channel flow largely through community arrangements often involving physical transportation of cash to Nepal. If Nepalese remittance service providers (RSPs) are allowed to enter into partnerships with Indian
banks and other regulated financial service entities in India to source
remittances, a viable mechanism can be evolved.

As can be deduced from this discussion, migration to India and remittance outflows from India are two important research areas for which

Figure A1.3   Recorded Outward Remittance Flows from India

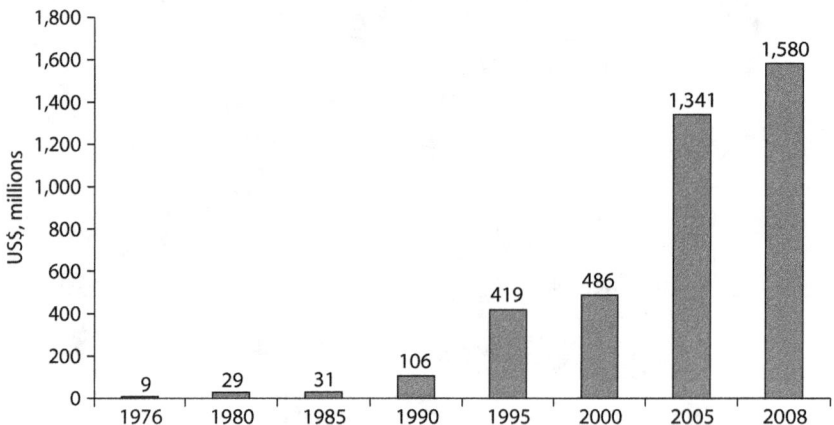

Source: RBI 2010.

information and data are limited and therefore merit further research and analysis.

Note

1. According to RBI regulations, an outward remittance can be repatriated in the form of foreign exchange by a foreign national (other than from Pakistan), not permanently residing in India, to his or her account or to a beneficiary situated outside India (except in Nepal and Bhutan) for those purposes approved under the Foreign Exchange Management Act (FEMA).

References

Kumar, A. 2008. "Bangladeshi Infiltration Reached New Territories." South Asia Analysis Group Paper No. 2838, September 11, Noida, India.

Reserve Bank of India. 2010. "NRI Deposits: Outstanding/Inflows and Outflows." Reserve Bank of India Bulletin, March 10.

World Bank. 2008. "Migration and Remittance Factbook." World Bank, Washington, DC.

————. 2009. "Migration and Development Brief 11." World Bank, Washington, DC.

Synopsis on Remittance Costs and Global Endeavors to Reduce These Costs

Remittance Costs: An International Perspective

Remittance transfers often can be costly relative to the low incomes of remitters and the small amounts involved, and they are not easily accessible. The costs of sending money vary and are influenced by several factors, such as the following: destination, transfer method, payments infrastructure, awareness and education levels of migrants, income levels, extent of market competition, and the prevailing rules and regulations. The World Bank's *Global Economic Prospects: Economic Implications of Remittances and Migration* (World Bank 2006) suggests that remittance costs have declined in recent years because of increased competition, use of technology in service provision, and government policies to improve transparencies in remittance transactions. In most corridors, particularly low-income corridors, remittance fees continue to be high, encouraging migrants to rely heavily on unofficial and community arrangements to send remittances.

The cost of sending remittances depends on both the source and destination countries. According to the World Bank's Global Remittance Price database (World Bank 2010), sending US\$200 from Singapore to Bangladesh will incur a modest charge of US\$4.50 or a 2.2 percent fee.

Sending the same sum from Australia to Papua New Guinea costs a whopping US$43.30, a 21.7 percent charge (see figure A2.1).

The cost of transfering US$500 from Australia to Papua New Guinea costs about US$76.20 (15.2 percent fee), while these costs are much lower at US$6.20 (just over 1 percent) from Singapore to Bangladesh (see figure A2.2).

In Latin America and the Caribbean, the costs of sending remittances have declined from more than 10 percent in 2000 to about 5.6 percent in 2005 (Orozco 2006). Evidence showed that higher aggregate remittance volumes, larger transaction amounts, lower exchange rate spreads, and increased competition reduced remittance costs. On the other hand, according to the International Fund for Agriculture Development (IFAD 2008), remittance costs to Africa are significantly higher than to other regions, reaching more than 25 percent of the remittance amount sent in some cases. Remittance transfers between African countries are particularly expensive. A recent study analyzing remittance fees across 119 corridors

Figure A2.1   Five Most Expensive and Five Least Expensive Country Corridors to Send US$200, Q1 2010

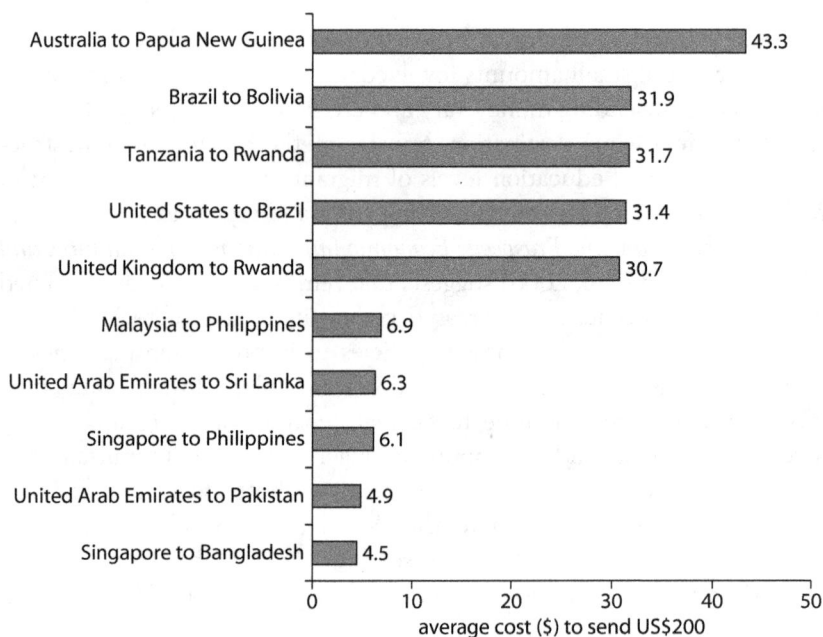

Source: World Bank 2010.

Figure A2.2   Five Most Expensive and Five Least Expensive Country Corridors to Send US$500, Q1 2010

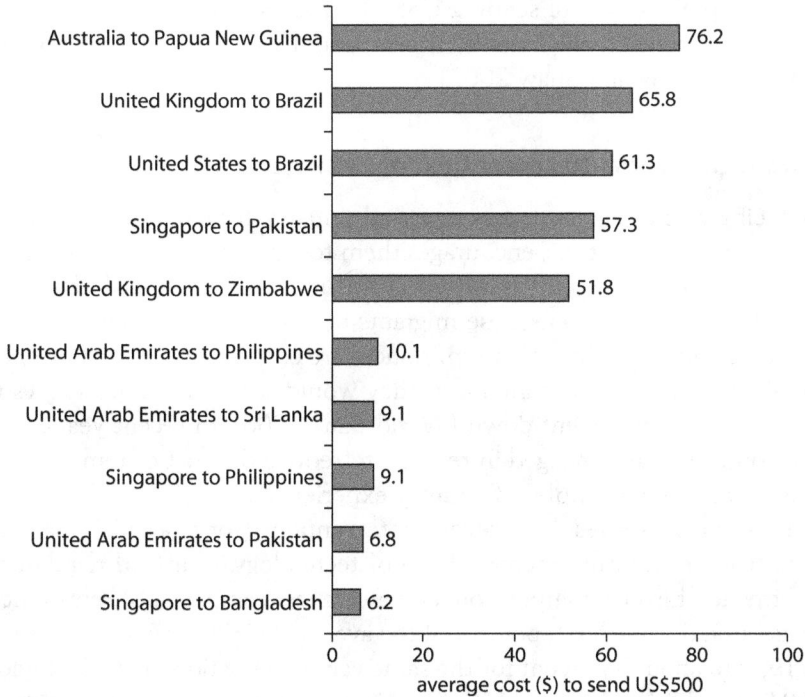

Source: World Bank 2010.

from 13 sending to 60 receiving countries suggests a positive and significant relationship between the migrant stock and average remittance fees across corridors. Furthermore, high-income sending and receiving country corridors exhibit high remittance costs on average, reflecting a high cost of nontradable goods such as services. Most important, the study finds that competition matters. Corridors with larger number of providers exhibit lower fees (Beck and Martinez-Peria 2009).

Finally, the costs of South-South remittances are usually higher than those of North-South remittances because of low levels of financial development, limited competition, and high foreign exchange commission at both ends of the transaction. South-South migration accounts for half of the total migration from developing countries and around 9 to 30 percent of developing countries' remittances inflows. Sending remittances from one developing country to another is more difficult, however, because in some countries migrants need to obtain authorization before central banks will process their international remittances. In addition, remittance fees vary significantly depending on the direction of the flow. For example, the cost of sending US$200 from Kuala Lumpur to Jakarta is about 6 percent, whereas it increases to 13 percent for the reverse direction (Ratha and Shaw 2007).

Global Endeavors to Lower Cost of Remittances

Reducing remittance costs has many advantages. It increases the disposable income of remitters, encourages them to send smaller amounts more frequently, and may shift remitters from unofficial to official channels. Survey results from Senegalese migrants in Belgium and Tonga migrants in New Zealand confirm that remittances are cost elastic. The majority of the survey respondents stated that they would send more remittances if the cost of sending went down (World Bank 2006). In recent years, several countries have engaged in reforms to reduce the cost of remittances. Below are a few examples of country experiences.

In Mexico, as a result of several interventions (for example, financial infrastructure reforms, increased use of technology, legal and regulatory reforms to enhance competition, and awareness campaigns),[1] remittance costs came down from 9 percent of the average US$300 value remittance in 1999 to about 3 percent for the same value transaction in 2005 (Taylor 2004). In addition, bilateral U.S.-Mexican efforts to promote competition in the market for remittance services and to bring those without bank accounts into the formal financial system have contributed to a dramatic decrease in the cost of sending (US$300) remittances from the United States to Mexico by about 60 percent between 1999 and 2005 (World Bank 2006). These efforts centered on the following:

- Improvements in the infrastructure—for example, by using credit cooperative networks as disbursement agents, through their interconnection to BANSEFI's *Red de la Gente* (see appendix C).
- Actions and incentives by the government, such as promoting competition and clamping down on monopolistic and exclusivity arrangements.
- Increase in transparency by requiring fees and exchange rates to be made public and prominent in remittance service provider (RSP) offices, and by consumer protection authorities producing and publishing comparative cost tables on a monthly (or even weekly) basis.
- Education programs to make migrants aware of their rights (including the possibility to open bank accounts with the use of the *Matrícula*

Consular) and of the several options available to remit transfers and their respective costs.

The Latin America and Caribbean Region as a whole has made important progress in reducing costs incurred by migrant workers in making remittance transactions through programs and initiatives of the U.S. government, Spanish savings institutions, the World Bank, and the Inter-American Development Bank's (IADB) Multilateral Investment Fund. These programs aimed at reducing the cost of remittances by stimulating competition among service providers, increasing awareness of remittance services, improving regulatory frameworks for financial services, and assisting microcredit and savings institutions in the region to design remittance-related products and services. In 2000, the cost of sending money to the region was in the range of 15 percent of the amount being sent (including a fee of around 10 percent, plus variable exchange markups of more than 5 percent). By December 2005, the average transaction cost paid by migrants to send US$200 to various countries in Latin America had dropped to 5.6 percent. Moreover, when taking into account that the average individual transaction amount is now US$300, the average cost incurred by senders is lower than 5 percent (Orozco 2006). Many reasons account for this decrease, such as the following:

- An increase in competition
- A growing interest on the part of banking institutions in the United States and Latin America in providing financial services, including remittances, to immigrants
- Tightened government regulations

For the Philippines, the cost of sending remittances home has been going down (substantially in some of the corridors) because of a combination of efforts to increase migrant workers' awareness as well as technological advances. According to an Asian Development Bank (ADB) study in 2006, the costs of sending money to the Philippines are now less than sending money to other South Asian destinations from Hong Kong SAR, China; Singapore; or Malaysia. Some of the reasons to explain this decrease include the following:

- The extensive use of mobile banking and sms to send money home by Philipino migrants, and the existence of the relevant infrastructure in the Philippines to accommodate this, spearheaded by reform of the central bank.

- With close to 1,800 rural banks throughout the Philippines, the Rural Bankers Association of the Philippines has launched RuralNet. Through RuralNet, the efficiency and security of remittances are enhanced, value-added financial and nonfinancial services are provided, and the government and private overseas cooperation is maximized (see box 4.2).
- Workers going overseas may attend a predeparture orientation seminar conducted by the Commission on Filipinos Overseas. This seminar program covers topics such as predeparture opening of a bank account, travel regulations, immigration procedures, cultural differences, housing issues, employment and social security concerns, and the rights and obligations of Philippine migrants.
- Finally, an initiative by the U.S. Treasury Department and the Philippines Ministry of Finance to reduce the costs of overseas remittance services (through greater competition and efficiency and enhanced access to formal remittance systems) resulted in a substantial decrease in the cost of remitting money from the United States to the Philippines.

Note

1. Some of these interventions were supported by the World Bank.

References

Beck T., and M. Martinez-Peria. 2009. "What Explains the Cost of Remittances." *VOX Journal*, September 28.

IFAD (International Fund for Agriculture Development). 2008. Remittance Forum, April 1, Rome.

Orozco, M. 2006. "International Flows of Remittances: Costs, Competition, and Financial Access in Latin America and the Caribbean—Toward an Industry Scorecard." Report presented at the meeting on "Remittances and Transnational Families" and sponsored by the Multilateral Fund of the Inter-American Development Bank and the Annie E Casey Foundation, May 12, Washington, DC.

Ratha, D., and W. Shaw. 2007, "South-South Migration and Remittances." World Bank Working Paper No. 102, Washington, DC.

Taylor, J. 2004. "Remittance Corridors and Economic Development: A Progress Report on a Bush Administration Initiative." Remarks presented at the Payments in the Americas Conference, Federal Reserve Bank of Atlanta, October 8, Atlanta, GA.

World Bank. 2006. "Global Economic Prospects: Economic Implications of Remittances and Migration." World Bank, Washington, DC.

———. 2010. World Bank's Global Remittance Price Database. Available at http://remittanceprices.worldbank.org/ (accessed April 15, 2010).

Mexico: Remittance Accounts

Mexico's L@ Red de la Gente (The People's Network), in cooperation with U.S. banks began its money transfer program in 2003 (Buchenau 2008). The goal of the program was to encourage more people to be banked. Currently, the People's Network has 122 member institutions that are mostly cooperatives (ranging from a few thousand members to more than 500,000). With more than 1,300 points of delivery in Mexico and more than 2.5 million members, the network has achieved a wide outreach in Mexico.

Description of the scheme and benefits to the account holder. Under this scheme, migrants can directly deposit money into accounts operated by a bank or deposit-taking financial institution in Mexico. The accounts are offered by a network of regulated microfinance institutions (MFIs) and cooperatives that use a platform run by BANSEFI (a public bank). BANSEFI also offers these accounts. The main benefits for account holders include the following:

- Account holders build a relationship with the account-holding institution that facilitates access to loans and other financial services.
- Deposits to accounts are available overnight, fees are significantly lower, and the exchange rate is better than for cash-to-cash remittances.[1]

- Withdrawal is convenient, especially in the case of institutions offering debit cards. If cards can be used internationally, then senders and recipients both have access to these accounts.

Types of accounts. Three types of accounts have been introduced under this scheme:[2]

- *Individual deposit account, accessed only by migrant:* These accounts are especially important for migrants, given the risks they face (for example, with regards to their legal status). Moreover, such accounts allow migrants to save for future investments. However, a limitation of this type of account is that these accounts have to be opened in Mexico; they cannot be opened abroad.
- *Individual deposit account, accessed only by relative or friend in home country:* The remittances received through this type of account reduces the risk faced by recipients as they can leave part of the money in the account. These accounts usually are used only by recipients to withdraw money. Usually, they do not accumulate larger balances.
- *Joint deposit account, accessed by migrant and a relative or friend:* Such accounts require a clear understanding between the sender and recipient about the handling of the account.

The opening balance required for these accounts is US$5.00. A key feature of these accounts is that they offer options to deposit or withdraw money without having to pay any fees. Migrants and their families usually prefer not to use account if monthly fees or fees on deposits or on withdrawals are charged.

The following accrue to the institution that is handling the remittance accounts:[3]

- *Growth of customer base:* Institutions offering remittances and remittance accounts have been able to increase the number of customers they serve.
- *Possibility to cross-sell other products that generate income for the institution:*[4] About 36 percent of remittance recipients have opened savings accounts (but save only a small portion and not yet regularly), while close to 7 percent of recipients at one institution have obtained loans for housing (which then had a good performance). In addition, some institutions have started to sell health insurance and life insurance products.

The following requirements must be met for the scheme to work:

- Accessible and appropriate locations for both senders abroad and recipients in home country.
- Strong marketing campaigns combined with financial literacy programs for both senders and recipients to help them set up and manage the accounts and any special features (for example, debit cards). Given the low level of exposure to financial services, appropriate marketing and financial education are essential to help migrants and their families make proper use of the services and overcome distrust against financial service providers (which in Mexico is strong after the banking crisis of 1995).
- Availability of a technological platform to manage transfers and deposits.
- Access to a national and international debit card network.

Notes

1. The fees for direct deposits are in the range of up to US$5.00, while cash-to-cash transfers have a cost of between US$8.00 and US$20.00 per transaction.
2. Diverse studies and experiences shared by migrants and Money Transfer Operators (MTOs) in the United States show that migrants have a strong interest in opening savings or deposit accounts in their home country and in their own name, given the often bad experiences they have had when asking relatives or friends to save money in their name. Many migrants would like to send money home, investing part into an account in their name and delivering part to their relatives. Joint accounts usually are difficult to manage.
3. Data are based on the study of one of the member institutions.
4. Because most remittance customers are unbanked, they usually start carrying out only remittance transactions and then, after some time, open accounts or request loans. The figures shown here refer only to accounts opened by recipients of remittances. Senders did not yet use the financial services offered.

Reference

Buchenau, J. 2008. "Migrant Savings and Alternative Investments." Presentation prepared for the Microfinance Summit, Nepal, February 17.

Model Remittances Customer Charter

Our Commitment to You, the Person Sending the Money, is the following:

Before agreeing to undertake a transaction, we will provide you with the following:

- An estimate of the total fee that you, the sender, will be charged by us for the transaction. If we believe that the receiver may also have to pay a fee, then we will tell you.
- An indication of the exchange rate that we will apply to your transaction. If a further exchange rate may be applied in the receiving location, we will tell you to expect this rate.
- Information on where the receiver should collect the money from and what he or she must do to collect it.
- Indication of when the funds will be available at the location to which you are sending them.
- Information on what you have to do if you want to cancel or modify the transaction and any charges for canceling or amending it.

Upon completion of a transaction, we will provide you with the following in writing:

- A transaction reference number that is unique to your payment.
- A security code or password for you to communicate to the person to whom you are sending the money.
- Confirmation of the exact amount we are sending for you.
- The fees that you have paid to us for this service.
- The estimated amount that the receiver will obtain and the currency that the money will be paid or credited in.
- The exchange rate that has been applied to your transaction in cases in which this information is available. In cases in which it is not available or in which additional rates will be used, we will tell you how the foreign exchange conversion will be calculated.
- Information on where the receiver can collect the payment or confirmation of the institution to which the money has been sent.
- When the money will be available for the receiver and whether this timeframe is definite or is the best estimate that we can make.
- In the case of cash collections, what the receiver has to do to collect the money.
- The procedure to follow if you need to make a complaint. We will tell you how long it will take us to provide an answer or an update.

If you are the person receiving a transaction, we will provide you with the following:

- A written receipt showing how much you have received.
- A transaction reference number that is unique to your payment.
- A note of any fees charged to you. We will not charge a fee unless the sender has been warned of this fee at the time the payment is made.
- The exchange rate that has been applied, if the sender has sent the money in a currency different from that which you will receive.
- In the case of cash collections, information on what documentation is required to collect the money.
- The procedure to follow if you need to make a complaint. We will tell you how long it will take us to provide an answer or an update.

Bibliography

Chanda, R. 2008. "The Skilled South Asian Diaspora and Its Role in Source Economies." Paper prepared for Institute for South Asian Studies at the National University of Singapore, Singapore.

Indian-Malaysian Online. n.d. Available at http://www.indianmalaysian.com/ (accessed on October 1, 2009).

NRI Internet. n.d. "NRI Population Worldwide." Available at http://www.nriinternet .com/Did_you_Know/NRIs_Population_WORLDWIDE/index.htm (accessed October 1, 2009).

OECD (Organisation for Economic Co-operation and Development). 2009. International Migration database. OECD, Paris.

Remit2India. n.d. Available at http://www.remit2india.tv/index.html (accessed March 1, 2010).

Reserve Bank of India. 2006. "Invisibles in India's Balance of Payments." *Reserve Bank of India Bulletin*, November 20.

University of Maryland. 2010. "India Human Development Survey." College Park, MD.

U.S. Federal Government. 2009. "U.S. Census Bureau Population Survey." Washington, DC.

www.ingramcontent.com/pod-product-compliance
Lightning Source LLC
Chambersburg PA
CBHW061751270326
41928CB00011B/2464